"I heartily recommend this book, . . . especially for those who are bogged down by old forms and irrelevant cliches"

—BRUCE LARSON

"The whole book moves along with persuasive power. It left me tingling from the shock of its briskness, warmed by the love it conveys and stirred by its honesty and truth"

—EILEEN GRUDER

"What a wedding of sentiment and sense! . . . The book has bite in it; it also has beauty"

—PAUL S. REES, *World Vision Magazine*

"This is Genie at her best"

—SHERWOOD E. WIRT, *Decision Magazine*

JUST
AS
I AM

by EUGENIA PRICE

TRUMPET BOOKS
published by
A. J. HOLMAN COMPANY
division of J. B. LIPPINCOTT COMPANY
PHILADELPHIA and NEW YORK

Published by Pillar Books for A. J. Holman Company
Printed in the United States of America

ISBN: 0-87981-055-6

Contents

Just As I Am

Just As I Am

1. Just as I am, without one plea,
   But that Thy blood was shed for me,
   And that Thou bidd'st me come to Thee,
   > O Lamb of God, I come, I come!

2. Just as I am, and waiting not
   To rid my soul of one dark blot,
   To Thee whose blood can cleanse each spot,
   > O Lamb of God, I come, I come!

3. Just as I am, though tossed about
   With many a conflict, many a doubt,
   Fightings and fears within, without,
   > O Lamb of God, I come, I come!

4. Just as I am—poor, wretched, blind;
   Sight, riches, healing of the mind,
   Yea, all I need, in Thee to find,
   > O Lamb of God, I come, I come!

5. Just as I am, Thou wilt receive,
   Wilt welcome, pardon, cleanse, relieve;
   Because Thy promise I believe,
   > O Lamb of God, I come, I come!

6. Just as I am, Thy love unknown
   Hath broken every barrier down;
   Now to be Thine, yea, Thine alone,
   > O Lamb of God, I come, I come!

Charlotte Eliott
1789–1871

1

Just as I am, without one plea, . . .

There is no necessity for pleading, no need whatever to make a case for ourselves with God. We are not the determining factor. God is.

Almost none of us seems to have this straight. Almost everyone attempts to be his own lawyer when he faces the Creator.

"I can't get through to God when I pray. I plead with him to help me, I plead for forgiveness, but nothing happens."

"I know all the religious routines, all the Scriptures on which to base my appeal. I have doctrine and I am sincere, but my spirit is cut from God's spirit."

"There must be something I'm not doing right. I pray. I read my Bible every day. I am active in the church, but my case before God is a weak one. Somewhere I am failing miserably."

"I plead with God to make me a more effective Christian. I try to explain to him where I have failed."

All wasted effort. All unnecessary. All based on the erroneous assumption that somehow, in some way, we need to explain ourselves to the One who created us in the first place. All slanted toward *us* as the determining factor in our relationship with God. All bearing on the efficacy of our case as we bring it before him.

In anguish and sincerity, sometimes simply, sometimes eloquently, before our own bar of justice we make our pleas and apologies for being as we are. We struggle to make it clear to the omniscient God that we are weak, selfish, jealous, dishonest, impatient, immoral, futile. Time after time we remind him that we are dust: prone to falseness and inconstancy, fickle, self-indulgent. We explain to him that our parents before us warped our characters by not loving us enough or by spoiling us or by setting up standards for us which we could not possibly reach. We plead with him to remember how many times our friends have let us down, how often our dreams have collapsed, how deeply we have been hurt. We may not mention our good deeds in so many words, but when we state our case we *feel* deserving in some areas, secretly expecting our virtues to stand us in good stead.

God is never unmindful of what we say to him or of what we think or feel in his presence. He is attentively mindful of everything about us. But this is not the point. The point is that we could be using this energy to act according to the truth about both God and ourselves, and our lives could be simplified and strengthened beyond belief. We could, if we *saw* the truth about God, begin to act in *his* energy, with peace replacing the anguish of defending ourselves before a nonexistent bar of justice.

We could use the effort spent in begging for mercy in a thousand creative ways; ways that would bring about our own healing, while we blessed and encouraged the lives of those around us.

In no way do I mean to imply that we have nothing to do. We have everything to do, but if our actions and our insights are contrary to the truth as anyone can know it in Jesus Christ, we waste, we dissipate. Most of us are active enough, but in the wrong ways.

God stands before us in Jesus Christ offering every grace, every power, every healing, every strength, every joy we need. "For it pleased the Father that in him should all fulness dwell." The all-encompassing need of every human being has already been met in Christ. He is there, available, waiting—even moving toward us, prodding us to receive. "Come unto me, all ye that labour and are heavy laden, and I will give you rest." Jesus Christ is not a religious theory concocted by the mind of man. He is the living God and he is there with you now, waiting for you to receive. Waiting for me to receive. Waiting for us to grasp the difficult simplicity of acceptance from his hands. But this kind of childlike acceptance has been made difficult by our own failure to believe the willingness of God. It has been made hard by our own tendency to complicate by futile and wasteful explaining, cajoling, pleading.

God, when he came to earth in the person of his Son, Jesus, did everything in his power to simplify. The ancient necessity for sacrificial offerings on our part was wiped out. God, himself, became the offering for us. God, himself, *came*. Came to us offering. His coming to live among us as God knocked over every barrier, opened the door to the holy of holies. Now, any man can not only enter the presence of the Lord God but also live there hour by hour, day by day, through every year of his earthly life. There are no specially anointed among us now: everyone is welcome. The door is open because Christ himself is the door. The gate to the Garden of Eden is no longer shut. We can go back to walk with the Lord God in the cool of the evening. We can be glad for his presence and never have to think of hiding again.

Forgiveness is abroad on the earth forever, now that Christ has come, and it is not for a select few, not only for those whom God has particularly called—God is calling everyone every minute. "He is not willing that any should perish." He is indifferent to no one. He is unmindful of no one. His back is turned toward no one. And he is confused by no one. God knows us *just as we are*. He knows you just as you are. He knows me just as I am. And once this begins to come clear, the futility of the "earnest plea" breaks over us. The foolishness of the lengthy explanation to the Father of why we are as we are, how we came to be this way, the extent of our limitations and our capabilities begins to appear ridiculous, even to us.

Of course, *we* need to learn about ourselves as we really are—as much as we can bear to learn—but we are not discussing the need for self-knowledge here. Anyone interested in a close relationship with God has already come to see enough of his own need if he is attempting to plead his case with the Father. Self-knowledge is necessary, but it can be disastrous unless one is simultaneously learning more about God. The sudden knowledge that we are spiritually proud, that we tend to boast "humbly" about our sacrifices, that we have been "using" God to build our own stock in any way, can be a devastation. Unless we see his hand in the new degree of self-knowledge. Unless we have learned enough about him to have come to expect forgiveness when we turn to him. To expect it at once, without pleading, without stating our cases. To expect forgiveness from him according to a kind of justice we ourselves have concocted. God never acts with us the way we think he should act. His justice is as far from our concept of justice as the east is from the west. God's justice (if indeed such a word can apply to him) is the justice of love. Our justice is the justice of worth: We are kind to those who deserve our kindness. We are merciful to those who we feel deserve our mercy, and we are merciful only as long as we think they deserve it. "His mercy endureth forever." And "he is kind to the just and to the unjust."

It is inevitable that our human sense of justice distorts our concept of God's love. There is little value in berating ourselves because we somehow feel we need to explain things to God in order to beg his favor. *We* are like this. We grant our favor to those who please us, to those who see things our way, to those who we feel deserve our favor. It is a natural tendency to humanize God. To think of him as being like us at our best. This is a *natural* tendency, but when we have any dealing with God we are dealing with the *supernatural*. He recognizes our nature as being the nature of man. He fully understands our natural tendencies. He is waiting for us to understand something of his nature too. True, God doesn't have to work at understanding us as we have to work at understanding him. He is God and

18

we are earth-bound people. But the earth-bonds begin to snap when we expend a little energy discovering for ourselves that the God of the Christian does not require self-improvement, does not require ritual, does not require good deeds or cultivated manners, does not demand strong faith and deep insights before he takes us to himself!

God welcomes us *just as we are* because he alone knows that we cannot change ourselves. To tell someone he must stop drinking, must stop lying, must stop being proud, must stop overeating and gossiping, before God will accept him is the most flagrant distortion of the Gospel of Christ. If we were living adequate lives, our relationship with God would be entirely different. In fact, those who for the time being think they are "doing all right" without a focused faith in God are impossible for him. He never breaks into a human heart. "Behold, I stand at the door and knock." God waits, *because* of his deep knowledge of us. He waits and never forces entry because he knows the nature of the true relationship possible between God and man. He knows the true potential of such a relationship. He knows that the only thing we must do is—come *as we are*. Then and only then can we begin to learn of him. Then and only then can we begin to grow, to mature, to gain the balance he longs to give each one of us. More about our part later. We must take the first step. We must *come*. But we can only come *as we are*, minus explanations, alibis—unpolished, empty of everything but the first, bright glimpse of the enormous potential of our life linked with God's life.

We must come entering no plea of our own, making no apologies for acting as any human being acts without God. To waste energy apologizing to the God who created us to live minute by minute in relationship with him, for acting wrongly *outside* that relationship, is ridiculous. He knows what the human heart is like without his control. There is a vast difference between being ashamed and being turly repentant. The truly repentant heart accepts the transforming power of the redeemer God. The heart making excuses for itself is admitting wounded pride: I am shocked and surprised and ashamed of myself for acting as I did. I really expected more of myself.

The plea for God's forgiveness based on fevered explanations (alibis) that our heredity or environment has been inadequate is likewise futile. After all, the human heart which receives Christ's forgiveness receives a new life too. The old home and family scars may remain, but "if any man be in Christ, he is a new creature." In the forgiveness of Jesus Christ—built right into it—is a chance to start living all over again. He does not offer merely the power to live a better life. He offers a *new* life. His own life implanted in ours. No one understands this but God. And no one can be expected to believe it until he has come to this God of love *just as he is:* without pleading his case, without begging for the mercy he has already been given, without first attempting to improve himself.

To expect to get oneself ready for God is to consider oneself an equal with God. And right here lies the source of the rest he offers: If we come just as we are, he will welcome us. Spiritual fatigue, a burdened heart, the ugly mess we make of our lives when we have directed them for years from a sin-distorted mind, cause us to long for rest—any kind of rest from the inner and outer tensions against which we struggle through our days. To expect such a troubled spirit to improve itself, to shine itself up, to untangle its own problems, is to expect the impossible. It is as impossible as to expect a man with two broken legs to sprint. He can't, and God knows it.

God offers the kind of inner rest that releases the energy we need to change our inadequacies to adequacies. We cannot do it for ourselves. We can read book after book with "help ladder" after "help ladder" explaining in detail how we can change ourselves, how we can overcome our problems, how we can create our own peace of mind. These books contain valued half-truths. Once one has entered into a personal relationship with Jesus Christ—once one has access to *his* power—these "help ladders" are useful. But I have never known anyone who could do the job alone. Jesus must have seen it this way. Otherwise he would not have extended his inclusive invitation to *all* those who were in particular need of rest, in particular need of a shared burden.

Two things are necessary for us: We must see our need and we must come. The rest is up to God. And he can move into action in our behalf much more swiftly if we come—just as we are. Making no alibis, no excuses, offering no explanations of how we got this way, expecting him to act—not according to our idea of one who sits in judgment—rather, *as he is*. And the Christian God has been proven to be a God of love. His is the love-motivated heart.

If we come *as we are*, expecting God to be there waiting *as he is*, we see at once that we are not the determining factor. God is.

2

But that Thy blood was shed for me, . . .

I cannot argue with the theology of this line from the old song. The only claim, the only plea anyone has with God is that He loved enough. He loved enough to be the God of the poured-out life. He did not wait for us to ask him to demonstrate the extent of his love; he broke into human history to give himself as proof. To "shed his blood."

To pour out his life.

Biblically speaking, *life* and *blood* are synonymous. Life and blood are synonymous physiologically speaking. No one who has, as I have, lost a loved one to the deadly disease of leukemia can ever doubt this. My father's blood cells *became* leukemia cells and his earthly life ended. The blood and life are one.

There are those who believe in some particular quality physically inherent in the poured-out blood of Jesus Christ on his cross. One author went as far as to claim that the chemical content of Christ's blood gave it a special power. Others (although their semantics tend to confuse me) contend that their "faith is in the blood of Christ." In the second stanza of the old song "Just As I Am," the writer speaks of the blood of Christ as cleansing every spot—each dark blot.

I do not think of my own cleansing in exactly these words, but I cannot argue with the theology behind them. If it is helpful to express one's faith as being in "the blood of Christ," if this is the way one came to believe, then I cannot argue. There is nothing to gain from demanding that the Great Act of God be worded in a certain way. I am sure God, as he hung on the cross, spilling his blood, did not concern himself with the doctrine of his act. He concerned himself, as he always concerns himself, with whether or not *we* were comprehending his love; were seeing *into* his heart; were grasping something of his all inclusive intentions toward us— just as we are.

It does not, it could not matter to God *how* we express his redemptive act on the cross, but it does matter eternally to him that we *communicate* it. If you tell me that your faith is in the blood of Christ, I would *now*—almost twenty years after my conversion to him—understand what you mean. And we would be agreed. Although if I were to attempt to communicate my belief, I would say that my faith is in Jesus Christ himself. Is this so different? No. Not to those of us who already know him. Not to those of us who have come to him—just as we were—and have found him there eager to forgive, to cleanse us, to make us whole, to start us on the way to eternal life right now on this earth. But if you had told me your faith was in the blood of Christ *before* I had come to him myself, I would have been confused, even repelled. Pages have been written on both sides of this issue—sadly, I think. Somehow, for some unexplainable reason, the blood of Christ causes hackles to rise. The Christian who attempts to speak in today's language fights mention of it. The Christian who has been conditioned to proclaiming that his "faith is in the blood" fights *for* frequent mention of it. Aren't both rather foolish?

God does not act within us in words and theories. He acts within us, to change and transform and unknot us, by his spirit. Both sides of this argument seem unlike the spirit of Christ. His spirit unites, heals, closes wounds, never causes them. Certainly Christ said: "I come not to bring peace, but a sword," but to use this profound statement of his as a hammer with which to bang the heads of other

25

Christians who choose to express their faith in different words is blasphemy. As with the white supremacist who quotes, also out of context, "Thou shalt not let they cattle mix with the diverse kind" as a "proof" that God is not in favor of integration among the members of the human race.

When Jesus said he came "not to bring peace, but a sword," he was not encouraging the brethren to fight among themselves over the way they worded their faith in him. He spoke of the sword that separates us to him in total devotion. He did not urge us to keep the division showing or ringing in our arguments. He merely said that those who do and those who do not believe in him will find a sharp line of separation between them. It seems to me he was stating an irrefutable fact. This does not mean that I am not to be friends, not to sit on the same platform, never to laugh with a non-Christian. It means that because I follow Christ I see things his way (or should) and not the world's way.

If those who refuse to mention the blood of Christ and those who insist upon mentioning it have both placed their faith in him as God and redeemer, their bitter arguments are useless—except to the enemy of God. I have met many persons who have claimed in a most superior fashion that their faith is "in the blood of Christ." I have likewise met many persons who have claimed in equally superior fashion that their faith is in Christ, but that they can't go along with this "slaughter house" concept of God's love.

I doubt neither of them where their sincerity is concerned, and it seems increasingly tragic that their concept of God is not strong enough to unite them around him. Is it *what* we believe about God that matters ultimately? Or is it that we believe *God?*

None of this is intended to shock, to imply approval of a swampy, uncentered faith in any superficial concept of God which happens to be convenient. Far from it. As God enlarges my own concept of him, my faith swings more and more certainly toward the fact of his poured-out life on the cross of Calvary. The fact of the necessity to me, personally, of that poured-out life. The fact of the necessity to you, of that same poured-out life—his blood.

Just as the old song declares: There is no other plea needed "but that Thy blood was shed for me, And that Thou bidd'st me come to Thee, . . ."

For me it is clarifying, faith-strengthening, helpful, to focus my attention on the heart and mind and nature of the Man-God on his cross. The blood he shed there was shed because of his intentions toward us all. The sight of blood means the sight of tragedy to us. We can grasp this. We cannot grasp—not ever on this earth—the full meaning of God's act on the cross, but we know there is tragedy connected with blood released from its normal life-giving course through the body. Something is wrong when blood is suddenly spilled. There has been trouble somewhere. When we give our blood to the blood bank, we feel we have given of ourselves. A kind of universal love is involved. We hope for the best, for new health for the person who receives it. Blood, the shedding of blood—the giving of blood—these things have meaning for us. God, in his written-down Word, uses terms that have meaning to the human mind. Jesus called himself the bread of life because everyone needs the life-giving elements in bread in one form or another. For this reason he called himself the bread of life. But it is even more important to me that everyone *likes* bread in some form. There were always many dimensions to everything Jesus said. He was not only claiming to be what every man needs, but what every man enjoys— once he has seen God as he is.

Even though God is God and nothing we can possibly do or say can diminish him in any way, his power, his love, his act on Calvary can be obscured by our attitude of heart toward those who do not express them in exactly the same way we express them. If I choose to say that my faith is in the God of the cross rather than in the blood he spilled on the cross, do you doubt my Christianity? Is the way in which you express yourself the basis for your salvation? Isn't God the basis? Isn't Jesus Christ the church's one foundation? Isn't the fact of his deity the rock on which he said he would build his church—his kingdom?

Does any of this diminish the blood he shed on the cross? Does it diminish his sacrifice? To me, it adds to Calvary. The fact that the blood spilled there was spilled because God chose to die for us, reaches my heart quickly. Bends my knees. Knocks down my barriers.

And for that reason, I can sing with my whole heart: "Just as I am, without one plea, But that Thy blood was shed for me, And that Thou bidd'st me come to Thee, O Lamb of God, I come, I come."

I can agree that Jesus Christ demonstrated the heart of the Father as he hung on his cross. And I can testify that my first dim glimpse of the truth that this *was* the Son of God hanging there, changed my life. Freed me from having to be agreed with in order to love. Freed me from feeling that somehow I have let God down when I don't manage to bring everyone I know into complete agreement with my way of attempting to communicate his salvation.

And there is that word *communicate*. God has bid us come—all of us. Are we letting this be known? I don't mean are we standing on platforms giving high pressure "invitations" while the congregation sings "Just As I Am." I mean are we communicating the heart of God? Are we daring to let him show us how wide his love really is? Are we courageous enough to be willing to be misunderstood as we speak out of the caring he has placed in our hearts?

I do not care much about you by nature. Before I came to the Lamb of God, I couldn't have cared less about anyone but a handful of special friends who happened to please me. Oh, I made contributions to worthy causes, but anyone can do that, and besides it's deductible. Caring, the caring of God, as we see it on his cross (for as long as we can bear to look) changes us first of all. His love shed abroad in my heart by the Holy Spirit causes me to care about you in a way I could never have cared before. But this caring changes me more than it can change you.

More and more I am convinced that I can communicate what I really believe about the poured-out life of God on his cross by permitting his love to change me in the wellsprings of my being: to stretch me, to make me tender and tough at the same time, to keep me reminded of you—to keep me reminded that I care about you because he cares about you and me.

If this seems to rule out human friendship and love, you have not got my point. Human friendship and love are inextricably a part of the suffering of Christ on his cross. He hung there feeling his life drain away, and he loved—not only universally, not only his enemies, but *particularly*. He singled out his best friend, John, and he singled out his mother, Mary.

I cannot consciously "sacrifice" for you even if I love you. If I love you, what I might do for you will flow from my heart because you are *in* my heart. I do not believe Jesus hung on his cross thinking: "Now, I'm sacrificing for them." He hung there pouring out his blood for us because we were *in his heart.* This does not mean he did not suffer. His agony drove far beyond anything we could comprehend. Not only did his body experience the torture of the most brutal kind of physical death, he did battle with all the selfishness and sin all men had ever committed or would ever commit. We cannot understand this. It is vanity to try. But this combined, two-pronged agony of body and spirit did not make him feel righteous. He *was* all righteousness. In the midst of his suffering, Jesus felt *natural,* because, to God, it is natural to love. The death of Christ did not change the heart of the Father toward us. The death and suffering of Christ *revealed* what the Father's heart had been like all along.

Does it bother you if I do not happen to express a point of theology as you express it? Don't you really care mostly that we both communicate the love of God in Jesus Christ so that for his sake, as well as for theirs, more and still more people will want to know him? After all, don't we forget half of the great loneliness when we think only of how much man needs God? Doesn't the cross tell us also that God needs man? Would he have gone to such lengths if he did not somehow need us? The Father created in the first place for reasons only he knows, but knowing him as dimly as we do now, we can be sure his basic motivation was the motivation of love. This is too difficult for man to believe: that God could love him enough to continue creation. Until Jesus came, few men, if any, had any real notion that the Father is a God of love. Merely because he was God and they were men, it was simpler to believe that he was a God of judgment—even vengeance. Something catastrophic had to be done and he did it in Jesus Christ. God *has done* the drastic thing on the cross.

He has done the one thing that can convince egotistical man that the only possible plea he has with God is the plea of love—love poured out for us in the poured-out life and blood of Calvary.

This God has bid us come.

3

And that Thou bidd'st me come to Thee, . . .

It is good always to be welcome, but the welcome of
God is almost more than man's mind can take in. It
is more than his mind can comprehend. Here, we
must depend upon our hearts. Our helpless, love-
starved hearts. When one is enduring the pain of
hunger, one eats when food is found, not question-
ing the source. One eats and discovers later. This is
the only way the human heart can cope with the
welcome of God. We can only "taste and see that
the Lord is good." We can only respond to his call
with our hearts and then permit our minds to catch
up.

The call of God to us to come to him will always seem a paradox. There are times when we all find ourselves in need of help—financial, emotional, spiritual. This is common to the human predicament. We begin at once to look around for that help. We call our attorneys or our best friends or our parents or our clergymen: "Help me," we plead. "I don't know which way to turn. I need your help." Perhaps the person to whom we have gone for help is able, perhaps not. Perhaps he is willing, perhaps not. This is the chance we take and we are aware of it. My mail frequently contains outright pleas for help. "I pray you can help me. I don't know anyone else to ask." Many times I cannot. I may want to, but I am unable.

Not so with God. There is never a question about his wanting to help us. He is the one who never stops calling to us. He is the one who calls, "Come!" Søren Kierkegaard wrote: "Oh! Wonderful, wonderful! That the one who has help to give is the one who says, Come hither! What love is this! There is love in the act of a man who is able to help him who begs for help. But for one to offer help! and to offer it to all! Yes, and precisely to all such as can do nothing to help in return! To offer it—no, to shout it out, as if the Helper were the one who needed help, as if in fact He who is able and willing to help all was Himself in a sense a needy one, in that He feels an urge, and consequently need to help, need of the sufferer in order to help him!"

Could this be one of God's reasons for creating? I do not see in this concept the necessity for believing that he *sends* suffering in order that we would call on him. I see, rather, a glimpse of the quality of his love: a love that is compelled of itself to help. A love that so hates our suffering that it thrives on urging help upon us. At times I glimpse God's heart as being so unlimited that he is never willing to wait for us to ask. This does not mean I see no need to pray, to importune. Rather, I see our importuning as coming from his desire to help us. Would we, if we are honest, really cry out for help to a God we thought would do nothing for us? To a God with whom we had no love relationship? Oh, man has cried out to "a god" since time began, but a faceless, loveless deity—until Christ came to give God content for us. There is a vast difference between crying out for help as into a void and crying out for help from a particular Person. A Person whom we know. A Person whose heart we know, whose intentions we know, whose willingness we never question.

God can only be known this way in Jesus Christ.

And "Oh! Wonderful, wonderful! That the one who has help to give is the one who says, Come hither!"

Calling for help from God through Jesus Christ does not diminish our suffering, our pain. Our grief is no less at the moment we cry out to him to help us, but help is there waiting. Grief, if it is real, may never be lessened—less sharp, but not lessened. God's help in those times comes in the way of new strength, new courage, new determination to avoid self-pity at all cost, as he avoided it on the cross. God's help comes in the offer of the power to over-come what has caused our suffering, rather than to make things all right again for us. If he brought all our loved ones back from the grave, spoke magic words to stop our pain instantly, he would make spoiled brats of us instead of sons and daughters of God. He always helps in the way *he* knows will be best for us, but he always helps.

And, Oh, wonderful! he is always urging his help upon us. No one ever needs to struggle to seek God. Does this shock you? Didn't Jesus say: "Seek and ye shall find?" Yes. But the very search is motivated by the One who longs to save us, to help us, to give us new life. No one ever needs to plead with God to come, and yet we do. We plead so loudly for God to "be with us," to help us, to save us, that we drown out his voice calling to us to *let* him help.

The One who offers help is the One (the only one) who has it to give.

The One who shouts, "Come!" is the Lord God himself, maker of heaven and earth and us. We do not need to badger him with pleas, and I believe we would soon stop if we could only be quiet long enough to learn of him. In our moments of adora-tion, our hearts and minds and spirits are over-whelmed with the wonder, the mystery that the

One who *offers* help is God. Can God care that much about one human being, we ask. Jesus says, "Yes," and we adore him and worship him and try to be grateful to him. But this is more likely to be during times of relative peace in our lives, during the so-called normal round, when nothing tragic has occurred.

What happens to us when suffering suddenly chokes our hearts? When some gigantic disappointment, some heartbreak so mutilates our peace that we know nothing will ever be the same again? It would be impossible for anyone to sit quietly adoring God, worshiping him in the usual way— meditating on his love—under those circumstances. But why does he seem suddenly so remote? Why is our suffering more real than the One who offers help?

One reason, surely, is simply the way our minds and emotions operate. What gets our attention gets us; and the new suffering, because it is painful and because it is new, has our attention. This is neither good nor bad. It is simply normal. But what about *after* the first shock has passed, the first torment lived through? Is God remote then? Is God still out of our reach? No. He is never out of anyone's reach because *he* is the one who reaches to us, but he *seems* out of reach when our hearts are breaking. Why is this?

Is it because we have never thoroughly laid hold of the truth about the *identity* of the Helper? We need to dwell on this: In our times of adoration, are we adoring our romantic concept of the seeking Saviour, or are we adoring him *as he is?*

Do we fall into the common trap of expecting God to be near when we are in a spiritual mood and not really expecting him when the roof of our world caves in? Do we dare to believe that God is there to help us only if, through some virtue of ours, some special recent generosity, we deserve him to be there? If we do, then we are missing the dynamic of the call of God!

God does not call us according to our response to him.

God does not call us according to our kindness or our generosity or our virtue or our church activity.

God does not go on offering his help because we have somehow earned it. *There are no conditions whatever tied to the love of God.*

If we need the best lawyer available, we know his assistance is going to cost more. If he is in demand, has a successful career behind him, wins the suit he handles for his clients, his fee is going to be high. We know this; we are conditioned to it. We expect real help to cost us something. The help God offers is totally free. There are no conditions, no fees, no "on demand" notes to sign. But because we are conditioned to expect to pay when we really need to be helped out of a bad spot, we insult God's holiness by bargaining with him. "Oh, God in heaven, if you will heal my beloved, I'll do this or that for You for the rest of my life!"

God does not love this way. His love does not operate on the repayment plan. He is not seeking a bargain from us. He is seeking *us*—to help us! The more successful a doctor or a lawyer, the more he feels his help is worth in payment. The more certain a man is that his professional services are going to meet the need, the more he charges. And yet God, whose services to us are always perfect, makes no charge at all. Neither do we need to seek him out, because he is forever seeking us to give us his help absolutely free.

Of course, this does not mean we owe God nothing. It does not mean he has no right to expect our love in return, no right to expect us to obey him. But here we need to examine the word "owe."

Does love ever really owe in return?

Love, as I am coming to understand it, gives, never expecting to receive in return. This does not mean that love cannot enjoy receiving. Here, again, is a paradox: Those who love give with no strings attached, are never insulted if they are not thanked. Still, those who love are freer than anyone else to enjoy the response of the loved one. As God enjoys our response. "He will rejoice over thee with singing." God rejoicing over us? Yes. But because he and he alone knows the innermost recesses of our hearts and our natures, he and he alone *knows* when we are "paying him back" or when we are responding to him naturally from hearts that love him enough to respond. I once gave a book to a friend, who in turn wanted to make a pie for me. When I said: "Oh, that isn't necessary. Love never owes anything," she disagreed. Love owes response, surely. And yet, is response, when it is spontaneous, like the payment of a debt? To me it isn't. And to my friend, the beautiful pie was a natural response. I truly believe that God can go up and down the aisles of any church on any Sunday morning and single out those who are "paying him back" by a conscious act of worship and those who are there responding to him just because they love him.

And that *thou* bidd'st me come to thee. . . .

It is good always to be welcome, but here the welcome overwhelms us because it is the welcome of God. It is *God* who invites us to come, with no conditions, no self-improvement, no perfect scores, no debt incurred. And equal with the wonder of the fact that God, himself, calls to us minute by minute to come to him for help is the wonder of the fact that he calls everyone—all of us. The most outgoing, helpful, well-intentioned, unselfish human being on earth would not sacrifice himself for *everyone*. The most unprejudiced among us is going to be a little choosey here and there with our favors. But not God. "Come unto me, *all* ye that labor and are heavy laden, and I will give you. . . ." God does not look for the well-bred, the deserving, the virtuous, the holy among us. He looks for everyone and he looks everywhere through every day and every night. His *is* a shepherd heart, the only one in existence. He is pleased when great numbers respond to him, but no more pleased than when one comes.

The Good Shepherd not only calls us, offering his help, he calls us to *himself*. Come to *me,* Jesus cries. And this cry is loud enough and insistent enough to reach the most wretched man alive, the man born in the lowliest surroundings. It is loud enough and insistent enough to reach the brain dulled with alcohol, the body dulled with too much food, the spirit surfeited with *things*. His voice is insistent enough and patient enough to reach to the dark depths of the tragedy-scarred heart. It speaks everyone's language and it never stops speaking of the love that heals and helps and frees. God is infinitely patient. He can wait. He does wait. Sometimes it seems that this is what God does most—wait. We are feverishly active in his behalf. We buy radio and television time and spend thousands of dollars propagating his Gospel, thinking of new ways to attract attention to it—even using cheap, emotional tricks. God does not. He just goes on waiting, but his waiting is not passive. It is active. It throbs and stirs with the motion of his eternal call to us: "Come unto me, *all*. . . ."

And he is calling us, not only to salvation or to sanctification or to become a part of his church.

His call is to himself. "Come unto *me*." He commands us to clothe the naked and feed the hungry and care for those whose material needs are great. But God does not stop with help in the form of new institutions and schools and food for the needy. He calls to himself, and only he can do this. He calls no man merely to service or to accept a certain doctrine. His call is personal, intimate, close. And only he can do this. Only God can really meet a man in that man's own innermost circumstances. Only God can adapt to change like this. Anyone can write a check or raise money for an orphanage, but only God can go to a human being where that human being is. Only God can go as low as the lowest human heart and keep his holiness unstained. Only God can go personally to the grieving and not be shattered by the shared sorrow.

More than that, God is not diminished by contact with us. We are saved by contact with him. We do not downgrade God. God lifts us up. The same God who bids us come to him for help.

"Oh! Wonderful, wonderful! That the one who has help to give is the one who says, Come hither!"

4

Just as I am, and waiting not,
To rid my soul of one dark blot, . . .

God's waiting is very different from ours. His waiting is creative, full of movement toward us. When we wait to come to him, our waiting is destructive, full of rebellion and pride. Full of movement away from him—toward more need.

We tend to think of "Just As I Am" as only an invitation hymn for those who do not know Christ. It is this, certainly. I read somewhere that more persons had listened to his call during the singing of this song than at any other time. The lyrics are quaint, early Victorian, but apt. For years they have intrigued me, have made me think beyond their somewhat forced rhyme to the rather amazing combination of both theology and psychology contained in them. I hope the old-fashioned melody runs through your mind as you read this book. It runs through mine as I write it—day after day. And my heart is called again and again. Even though my own first turning to Jesus Christ was not in a church or even in a meeting of any kind—the old melody and the lyrics cause me to remember.

It *is* a song for those who feel, who recognize the tug of the first call from God.

It is a song which identifies with the conflicts, the fears, the doubts, the feelings of unworthiness. The stark aloneness of the spirit at having first seen itself cut off from all of life as long as it is cut off from God. Then the first feeble move toward the light is made. The recognition of one's need. The hope of help to come. There is joy in it too, because there is affirmation before God. But there is also sadness . . . the kind of particular sadness one knows at the moment of turning. Joy because God will be there when the turning is made, but also sadness that we have waited so long.

And there is searching.

But the searching is not ours. It is God's. We are drawn to him because he is drawing us. We are finding him because he has found us. Suddenly we know the shepherd heart has been at work on our behalf all the time. The darkness is about to go, but

44

it has been there so long we almost fear the light ahead. We dare not wait and yet we do.

For three days nineteen years ago he called to me while I waited, held back, tried to understand with my mind. There was, during these days, a lull in life around me and a restlessness and a waiting that was full of sadness and joy. It was as though I knew something eternal and tender was about to happen. Still I waited, feeling at once strange and familiar with this God who had never before existed for me. And who now seemed to surround me. I had not turned to him, I had not asked forgiveness, but the Holy One of Israel had my attention, my full attention. The sadness and the joy were all around me and the kindness. I went to church for the first time in over eighteen years that Sunday, and although I didn't remember to include it when I wrote the story of that time in *The Burden Is Light,** I now recall sharply, as I write this book, that during the Holy Communion that morning, the organist played "Just As I Am." I hadn't heard it since I was a child, but these lines came back to me:

> . . . *and waiting not*
> *To rid my soul of one dark blot.*

I ended my waiting at last. And that bright, definite moment of turning—the struggle over—comes back to me still when I hear the old melody.

* Westwood, N. J.: Fleming H. Revell Company, 1955.

The lyrics of "Just As I Am" seem written for the person who is being compelled to come for the first time, but if we leave the song at that, those of us who have already come miss much. It is for us too. Actually, if we stopped to recognize what is here for Christians as well as those moving into faith, we might find there is even more for believers than for nonbelievers.

"I keep trying so hard to be a good Christian. I'm almost sure God has received me as his child. I know he would for certain if I could stop this or that."

"I envy anyone who has joy in his Christian life. Although I suppose, if I could turn to curb my temper, God could bless me, could give me joy. Honestly, I'm *trying* to curb it. My temper and my tendency to gossip."

Trying.

Trying to "rid my soul of one dark blot" or another.

Have you paid attention to the second stanza of "Just As I Am"? The secret of the growth in the Christian life is all here:

> Just as I am, and waiting not
> To rid my soul of one dark blot,
> To Thee whose blood can cleanse each spot,
> O Lamb of God, I come, I come!

We tend to think so superficially in this area of our spiritual pilgrimage that we insult the God who created our minds. Who can rid himself of one dark blot? Who decided that these words applied only to sinners who need initial repentance and salvation? Who doesn't need both all the time? How dare we limit God like this? How can so many sincere, well-meaning, earnest Christians go on *trying* to become something they're not ready to be? Do we heap false guilt on one another's head by all our preaching and writing and lecturing on what *we* think to be the standards for God's sons and daughters?

Somewhere, from someone other than God, we have got hold of the whiplash of self-effort, and we use it on ourselves and on each other unmercifully. Not only without mercy, but with stupidity—or at least blindly. Where do we get the idea that only the "unsaved" need to cry, "O Lamb of God, I come, I come!" Don't we all need to come to God for help every minute of our lives? I refuse to be boxed in by doctrine here. We are not speaking primarily of the soul's initial need for the saving grace of God. I believe in the need of the *saving* grace of God in everyone's life, but I believe equally in the *helping* grace of God.

As soon as some of us run up against a previously unrecognized or hidden sin in our hearts we begin to doubt that God has saved us in the first place. Or, worse yet, we are surprised at ourselves. So surprised, we attempt to hurry up and "rid our souls of [that] dark blot" fast before anyone else catches on that it's there.

"I was born again many years ago and have been active in Sunday school and church work all of my life. I am the one who is called on for devotions in the women's meetings etc. But I feel so cold toward God most of the time that I am about ready to leave the church altogether."

This woman may have wanted to hit me when she read my answer to her letter. I told her simply that it seemed to me she needed to come to God. I then quoted a stanza of "Just As I Am" and signed my name. I didn't know what else to say because she was a victim of the common belief that Christians just go along having their devotions and serving and never need to make a single other move toward him. Too many of us appear to feel that we've done God the initial favor of coming in the first place and now it's all up to him. In a sense it is all up to him. But what we don't see clearly enough is that we didn't come to him that first time—he came to us!

God alone can cleanse the spots we keep finding in ourselves, but even he cannot do it until we come for cleansing. He is not waiting for us to work on improving our spiritual appearance—our Christian image; he is waiting for us to come to him for cleansing. When God removes a spot, it doesn't come back. We can restain, but his cleansing is thorough.

None of this is meant to suggest that we need not use the self-control which God gives us. But self-control is of little permanent value until the self is under the control of the God who created it.

"I'd become a Christian if I didn't have to stop doing so many things first."

Who said we did? Jesus said we were to come to him weary, burdened, in need. He put a little child in the midst of his listeners and said we were to be like the child when we come to the Father. Eager, not reluctant to say what we need. Eager to be cleansed, not ashamed that we need it.

With permission I want to share a portion of a long, long letter I received some time ago.

> I can write all this to you because I do not know you personally and probably never will on this earth. Also, I am ashamed to confide to any of my friends. Least of all, would I even think of telling my minister.
>
> You see, I am a member in good standing (so far as the church knows) of the board of deacons. I have been active in my church and supported its work with my money and my time for many years. I am a man fifty-five years old, am married and have three grown children.
>
> For the past five years, however, I have been living a double life. The church secretary and I worked together on church projects for sev-

eral weeks before I realized that I was in love with her. I don't expect you to believe this, but I did love her in a way I had never loved my wife. We were married too young, before either of us were mature enough for marriage and before either of us knew what the other was really like. But the years passed by, our children came and grew up and I didn't realize what I was missing until I came to know the woman who seemed to understand me better than I understood myself.

After two or three pages of details, the letter goes on:

This woman and I have been intimate, stealing every possible hour together now for five years. Until a few months ago I managed to kid myself by pretending to thank God that I had at last found someone who really loved me and believed in me. I know I was kidding myself because now I can't pray. I fake headaches to miss church for fear I'll hear something in the sermon (or direct from God) that will make me even more miserable than I am.

I can't give her up and I can't go on like this. Would you advise that I divorce my wife and marry her? Of course, I'd have to leave the church and I suppose God would leave me. Maybe He has left me already. There certainly seems to be a space between us all the time now.

I'm going to mail all of this because if I read it over I won't send it. But in the paragraph above I wasn't honest. I am *not* asking you if you think I should divorce my wife and leave the church in order to marry the woman I love. I know I can't do that. Maybe I really don't want to after all. But what I do need to know is what do I have to do to get God to take me back? If I stop seeing her, will He talk to me again? Will He forgive me? How can I go to Him at all until I stop this thing I am doing?

My heart went out to this man. His suffering is very real. And if my heart went out to him whom I had never even seen, how must God's heart be reaching toward him to help him? I could only tell him that if he goes to God *as he is,* God will show him and he won't need me. "How can I go to Him at all until I stop this thing I am doing?"

A tragic, pointed instance of the Christian *waiting* to rid himself of a spot which only God can cleanse.

Where indeed do we get the idea that we have to *be* a certain way, in a certain state of virtue, in a certain state of worth, before God will meet us? Did Jesus Christ come to earth to save holy men? No, He came to save sinners. Isn't it mainly human pride that causes us to get so far off the track in our thinking about God? Aren't we expecting ourselves to be fairly first-rate people on our own? Oh, we profess salvation by Christ, but when we insist that we have to polish ourselves up before we can appear before the living God, we are insisting that he is not a God of love! We seem also to be insisting that some part of our salvation is up to us. We are calling ourselves little saviours every time we wait to rid ourselves of something before we feel "worthy" to come to him. More than this, we are implying that we are the only ones who know about the "dark blots."

Doesn't God know too? Doesn't he know us better than we know ourselves? Better than we could bear to know ourselves?

The One who is the Helper is calling to us all to come and come again *just as we are*. This is the great comfort, the great relief. There is no relief more complete than to discover, at last, something of what God is really like.

And there are no exceptions to his call. It is to everyone who needs him, and this is everyone, everywhere, under every circumstance.

5

**Just as I am, though tossed about
With many a conflict, . . .**

When we think of conflict, we think of discord, a
battle between two opposing forces or sets of ideas:
between two loyalties, two authorities, two sets of
conditioning. We feel turmoil in the word itself. In
"conflict" there is no hint of rest or peace or creativity. One side fights the other, often to a stand-
still. The whole of life is interrupted, pushed forward by the impetus of one side and pushed back
by the impetus of the other. Hostility is present and
a struggle for mastery.

That this often agonizing striving for mastery

53

takes place in the soul of the man or woman approaching God for the first time is well known. I have experienced it. So have you, if you have made a definite move toward him as an adult. Jacoblike, we do battle with the Lord God. Our hearts long for him, our circumstances and the emptiness of our lives without him (seen suddenly or known for a long time) cause us to want to run back to the Father's house. Into each one of us was created the need, the capacity to be at home with the Father. He created us for himself, able to enjoy him, to live with him at peace. He created us in such a way that we can know no peace anywhere outside the Father's house. And yet, when the time comes for us to make the last turn in the road that leads there, the conflict begins. In one sense, it is a conflict within us: between our two natures. The real nature presses forward toward home; the false nature does battle every step of the way. We know there is plenty with the Father; plenty and joy and peace and eternal life. Up ahead is all we were created to enjoy, and yet the side of us which has ruled up to now, which has thrown all the cues, has been our master, begins to fight for its very life: the life lived as *we* want to live it, not as God intended us to live.

The battle rages as long as we want it to rage. It ends when we choose to end it, because we are in control of our wills. It is true that God does not stand aside leaving us to do battle alone. He is there too, but he never strives with our real natures, only the false, the destructive, the superficial. His weapon is love and it never kills, but always makes alive. He fights on our side, although it does not seem that way while the battle rages.

We are "tossed about" in every sense. Our feeble arguments sound even to our own prejudiced ears like the babblings of a drunken idiot. Even as we fight the love of God, we feel foolish, longing for it in the midst of the conflict. We may even wonder as we struggle why we don't give up and take the rest he offers, and yet the fight goes on.

And it goes on as long as our false (self-occupied) nature chooses to make its alibis, to set up its arguments. We say to ourselves: I might like being with God, but I can never like being with church members! I could never acquiesce to fellowship with those who have it all settled and who would not welcome me.

But then God wins a point: Down deep inside we know *he* does welcome us and he welcomes us *just as we are.*

Still unbeaten, our self-concerned side tries again: If I become a Christian, how can I operate my business? I will have to make restitution not only with my money but with my pride. I cannot face this or that person and admit to what I have done again and again all through my adult life. This is too much. I will fight to the death.

Again God makes a move: You do not have to do any of that alone if you take my yoke upon you. I will be there making restitution with you, giving you my courage, my grace.

God's enemy regroups and tries again: But what would life be like if I had to do as these Christians do? What fun would there be if I gave up this and gave up that?

The steady eyes of Christ look back at us and even though he says nothing in so many words, we know suddenly (that is, unless we are doing battle with conformist Christians instead of with God) that he does not expect us to break any habits, change any patterns of thought, alter any pleasure *alone*. If we have anything resembling a clear concept of God's intelligence, we will refuse to accept the inferior intelligence of the moralists who lay down the laws. We plunge toward and then jerk away from the sure conviction within us that God works another way—from *within*, never from *without*. Perhaps, we think frantically at first, if I just start giving him the controls, just begin to live my daily life with him, *he'll* change my desires. We sense we have, on this thought of ours, moved a big step closer to God.

The conflict goes on as long as we choose. And God is never in a hurry to end it. People are, because they think they might add a new member to the church. But God wants this conflict to end forever when it ends. He is never in haste about bringing it to a climax. He will go on for years if necessary to see his child through to freedom. He is no more interested in seeing us chained by conformity to a religious group than he is in seeing us chained by conformity to our sinful natures. He wants us *free*.

This battle, this conflict can be violent or it can go on almost unnoticed by anyone outside. God calls everyone to himself, not just the flagrant hedonist, not just the obvious "sinner." I have watched the same battle rage in a quiet, ladylike manner within the heart and mind of a cultivated suburbanite who did battle with God over her unwillingness to love her mother-in-law. But God's battle tactics remain the same: he loves and stands firm and waits. Not because he has to prove his Lordship—why should he? That is an established fact. But because he loves. And love always wants peace for the loved one. God sees the futility of our battles waged against him with more clarity than we could ever see them, but he is also a realist. God is more realistic than we could bear to be. He sees things as they are, and he sees us as we are, and this is the only surrender agreement he has drawn: that we come—just as we are. Until we do—he waits, but with his love always moving toward us, never away.

The familiar conflict that rages within the very being of the person making his first surrender to God is not the only conflict. Truthfully, once this initial surrender is made, another kind of conflict begins which may cause the first one to seem like a skirmish. And this conflict may go on indefinitely.

It does not need to go on, but it often does. This is the battle of the Christian learning to live the Christ-life in the midst of unsympathetic friends, unsympathetic members of his own family, an amoral, secular society—in the midst of what often appears to be a veritable new attack from some secret enemy.

I hope I will be rightly understood when I declare that much of this apparently new conflict is unnecessary. Much of it is created by our ignorance of what the truly Christian life is really like. And this kind of ignorance is normal for the new believer. He has not yet had time to learn of God. Until we know God's nature we have no idea how that nature operates in us. We cannot know the Christian viewpoint until we know the viewpoint of God himself. We cannot know the viewpoint of God until we know God. Too many overly enthusiastic religious groups "convert" people to their way of life, to a "new *way*" of life, thereby blocking God's offer to *give* scott-free, an entirely *new life*.

I receive agonized letters from sincere new Christians who smoke. The members of their religious group keep them reminded that "when they reach a certain stage of holiness" they won't think of doing such a sinful thing! The "faithful" keep them reminded that they are being prayed for because on this one point they are in rebellion against God. What these well-meaning Christians are really doing is forcing the new convert to keep himself and not God in the center of his attention. Here again, the old truth: What gets our attention gets us. The new believer, instead of experiencing the inner release and joy of forgiveness, is kept guilty and self-conscious because in one area of his life, he is still self-indulgent. Of course, there is never one member of the praying group who is in no area self-indulgent. Excessive smoking *is* self-indulgent. So are excessive eating and excessive talking and excessive criticism. These good people quote Scripture by the yard and skip the personal application to the beams in their own eyes. All of us have a tendency to read into the Scriptures what *we* want to find there. The folk who center on the doctrine of eternal security can give you a dozen "proof texts." Those who build their doctrine around the *danger* of the doctrine of eternal security can also give a dozen "proof texts." Those who stand firm for one particular method of baptism can supply Scriptural "proof" for their stand. The list goes on. But what might happen to the new Christians and the old if we all began to read our Bibles with two goals and two goals only in mind: To find out more of what God in Jesus Christ is really like and to discover what he has to say to us as individuals?

When I first came to work for my present boss, he led me to Jesus Christ. I thought he was the greatest man I had ever known. I joined his church and began to go regularly to a Bible class he taught. That I found a new life in Christ, I have never doubted. I still have everything to learn and I, of all people, know it. But my conversion was three years ago and during this time some of the glow has worn off my boss for me. He watches me like a hawk to be sure he is "exhorting" me properly and yet the other day when I was forced to ask him a question concerning some of his business ethics, he blew his top! Among other things he could not see at all that it was a matter of morality that he "retired" an old and faithful employee seven months before this man would have received his pension from my boss' company. He actually reminded me of the "beam in my own eye" *and* for the hundredth time that he had been the one to lead me to Christ. This seems somehow to make him special. As though he deserves some sort of special homage from me. I don't feel that way. Am I so far out on this?

I would say this young woman is on dead-center. And I congratulated her that she had balance enough *not* to permit this man to cause false and unnecessary conflict in her. She had gone to God with the problem first before she wrote to me. He had set her straight. There was nothing left for me to do but offer congratulations. Her shallow-thinking boss could go to God too, but of course, the poor fellow feels he already has. After all, isn't he a soul-winner? And doesn't he teach the Bible class in his church? I doubt that he is close enough to the heart of God to have any conflicts. He is well-versed in the Scriptures and can give you his doctrinal statement in a flash, but more is required. I do not question the man's salvation. I would question God if I were to do that. Salvation is God's part, but I do question, because I am forced to, that this young lady's boss *knows* God. In the boss's case, some conflict would be helpful and healthful.

God never resists our conflicts. He welcomes them. They can drive us to him as nothing else can do. Of course, they can drive us away too, but this is for us to decide. If we want to be really free of conflict in any situation, over any point whatever, we will go to God. We will respond to his invitation to us to come to him though "tossed about with *many* a conflict, . . ." His welcome never varies. It is never dependent upon our spiritual state.

A minister once said to me: "I wish I could pray about this conflict of mine, but I can't. I tell my people to do it, but for myself, I just can't reach the point of being able to confront God with it. I'm too ashamed."

This man knew God's invitation covered his need, but I could only conclude that he just didn't know God himself well enough to feel free to respond.

Have you ever stopped to think how foolish we are to act as though God knew *nothing* of our conflicts, our inner battles? As though we and we alone knew?

There are times when we miss creative fellowship with him because we refuse to discuss a conflict in his presence until we are ready to resolve it. Until we are at least ready to do all we can to resolve it. I have done this, and invariably I found myself avoiding direct contact with him in other areas too. My side of our relationship cooled. I believe it to be indifference toward his sacrifice on the cross when we ask for forgiveness with half our hearts. Forgiveness cost God too much for us to make a mere ritual of it. A fetish. To take it lightly just for the sake of temporary relief for us. There is only danger in not discussing *everything*—all our conflicts and our stubbornness and rebellions with God. There is only danger in *not* talking it all over with him—just as it is. If we are unwilling to let go of a thing or a person or an attitude, it is better to be honest with God and ask him to show us how to let go. Or to make us willing to be willing. He knows anyway. If he knows about the sparrows, certainly he knows about the battle raging in the hearts of his children.

And he waits, but as he waits, he urges us to come to him—just as we are, dragging our conflicts along with us.

6

. . . many a doubt

The man or woman who has not yet entered into a personal relationship with Jesus Christ quite understandably *doubts*. He or she does not know God and it is difficult to have *active* faith in someone we do not know. And, of course, the initial leap of faith is required before we can know him. We must decide to try it out—to discover for ourselves if he is really there as he claims to be. If he is who he claims to be. None of us knows anything for ourselves until we accept it as true, or until we try it.

The new Christian is often besieged by doubts

soon after conversion. This is to be expected, simply because the first glow of discovering God dims after a while and if faith has been based on the first *feeling* of high exhilaration, doubts take over. I was one of the fortunate ones. I was amply warned that nothing whatever in my experience with God was dependent upon the way I *felt*. From the start I had it straight that my periods of joy did not necessarily mean I was advancing. Nor did my periods of depression necessarily mean I was retrogressing. Both merely meant that I, like every other human being on earth, am affected by my emotions. And emotions change as the weather changes. The sun, like the Son, remains even when it's storming.

God is totally acquainted with human doubt. More than that, he knows thoroughly all the causes for human doubt. He is never shocked by doubt. He expects it and he knows exactly how to cope with it. Our part, as I see it, is to go on as though we didn't doubt. This does not give escape from the inner turmoil that inevitably accompanies doubting, but it does exercise our faith. And faith is our part. We decide whether or not God is reliable and our faith grows especially during those times when we *act* positively toward him while feeling our most negative—our most doubtful.

We tend to understand doubt among new believers or nonbelievers, but almost never among those who are supposed to have come a long way up the road of faith. We are shocked and troubled and disillusioned when someone whose Christianity we admire is suddenly a victim of doubt. This shows, of course, that we are leaning on someone else's faith rather than upon God. A stupid waste, but we all do it in some measure. And in so doing we are cruelly unfair to those whose faith we trust more than we trust Christ. I am not alone in cringing when someone appears to place confidence in my faith. This happens with anyone in any area of Christian public life, and it is unfair to us all. We are merely on the way, along with everyone else. We have no corner on uninterrupted sanctity. We are people too. And all people know periods of doubt. Some of us are born doubters. Others, like myself, who knew love all through childhood and who find it easy (not virtuous) to believe, know less doubt or shorter periods of it. But we all experience it whether we consciously recognize it or not. Whether we have been made humble enough to admit it or not.

Doubt is nothing for which we should be ashamed. It is natural to us all. But it is something which we can learn to overcome, and we learn by coming to understand some of its causes.

Perhaps the most obvious causes should be looked at first.

Rebellion can nourish doubt more quickly than any other state of mind. Our rebellions are often due to actions of our own, but not always. They come crowding in upon us when things around us go wrong, when someone we love dies, when we unwittingly fail, when we are let down by a friend, when we are deeply disappointed by anything or anyone. We fight all of these circumstances. This is human nature. We can find no possible reason why this thing should have happened to us. Here, of course, we expose our unconscious faith in *karma* and not Christianity. Jesus did everything in his power to show us that we are not blessed or hurt according to *our* virtue. "In this world you *will have* tribulation. . . ." In the period of history covered by the Old Testament, man, because Christ had not yet come, believed that God prospered a man according to his faithfulness to God. When Job's world crumbled around him, all of his friends tried to tell him that he had somehow brought it on himself. Job did not have the light we have now, but he clung to God—willing *not* to understand. We now know that God does not "reward" us with material blessings or happy surroundings. We now know, because of Christ, that God gives himself and peace in the midst of turmoil. Still we begin to doubt God, to rebel when our happiness is disturbed. Only those who have accepted the truth that happiness is not the end can bear *not* to be rebellious. Only those who have learned that nothing that can happen can change the *joy* of God. Happiness and prosperity *and* joy in God are not the same. We tend to make them synonymous, but they are not.

Continued disobedience also breeds doubt. When we go on disobeying once we have seen our mistake, the pressure must go somewhere and so the human tendency is to put it onto God: to begin to doubt him. Prolonged disobedience to God leads invariably to tricky rationalization on our part and this tricky rationalization most often ends up in our cry of doubt. Somehow we feel relieved of the responsibility for our misdoing if we can say we doubt. After all, we rationalize, if I don't really have God straight any more—if I am overwhelmed by doubts, then I'm really not in a frame of mind to obey him, am I?

Less obvious cause for doubt is the frighteningly common feeling of *superiority* among us. The moment we begin to feel superior to anyone (and who never experiences this?) we can be heading for a period of doubt. The basic reasoning here seems clear: Only God is superior and when we feel our own superiority and begin to act on it, we are doing exactly what our first parents did in the Adam and Eve story. We are grabbing at the first opportunity to play God. Now, I do not mean to imply that we are all of us equal intellectually, spiritually, or even emotionally. Some persons, through no merit of their own, are born with superior intellects, superior spiritual capacities, deeper emotions. The point here is that we can be moving toward doubt of the Father when we begin to *feel* superior to our fellow man. When we begin to *act* as though we know it all. "Pharisaism" is the popular nasty label used to attach to the self-righteous individual who has it all figured, who almost dares us to suggest he could be wrong—the very spirit which gripped the Pharisees in Jesus' time and drove them to crucify him. The Pharisees had spent their lives studying and interpreting the Scriptures. They based their eternal salvation on their *knowledge* of God's law. They had it all decided, and anyone who dared disagree with them they would wither, silence—or, in the case of the Son of God, attempt to eliminate. There appears the same steely spirit within us as appeared in the Pharisees when we mount out spiritual pedestals and let it be known by our words or our attitudes that *we* are the authorities.

But those of us who deprecate, look down upon, or despise others in whom we see what we call a pharisaical attitude are as guilty as they! And of the same thing—feelings of superiority. I have been slow to learn this. For years I despised the doctrine clutchers who hardened at the first sign of disagreement and I felt myself being filled with what I called, "righteous indignation." Inevitably, as I look back, during those periods when I was in particular rebellion against the i-dotters and t-crossers, I was also in periods of what I can now recognize as doubt. Jesus warned us amply about this: "Judge not that ye be not judged." There is a fine line between perceiving the fact of an unchristian attitude or a failing in another and actually judging the *person*. As nearly as I have been able to define this line it seems to me that when I am merely perceptive, have caught an unchristian characteristic in someone, I am personally not affected one way or another in my appraisal of myself. I do not feel superior simply because I have sensed a fault in someone else. This is not judging, in my opinion. But, when I run headlong into a flaw in someone else's character and Phariseelike stand back and feel proud that I do not share the same flaw, I am judging. We would never have to work to obey God's command not to judge each other if we kept our own records clear, if we kept constantly before us all that God has had to do for us, all he still has to do for us.

Another less obvious cause of doubt is *ingratitude*. Paul told us we were to give thanks in all things—right in the middle of trouble we are to be thankful. There is no more difficult admonition anywhere in the Bible, but neither is there a more productive, creative one. Because hidden here is the key to the constantly open heart. A grateful heart simply cannot snap shut. Its lock is permanently broken. And any heart steadily open to God cannot doubt him. It seems easy for us to concentrate upon and believe in the reality of our troubles, our problems, the people who wrong us, our physical and emotional pain, our heartbreaks, our anxieties. These are real to us with no effort on our part. And it seems beyond us to give thanks for such harsh realities. Slowly or swiftly, depending upon the number of our troubles, we begin to lose the sense of God's reality. He is overshadowed by all that is wrong in our lives.

How to get back to the reality of God? Imagine that our troubles are not there at all? Nonsense. Think them out of existence? Impossible. We can only begin, however feebly, to give thanks to God whether we feel thankful or not. If we can't thank him for our problems, we can at least thank him for something good in our lives: two legs on which to walk, two eyes with which to see, a stomach with which to digest our food, hands with which to touch our loved ones, books to read and music to hear and trees and sky and water and rain and sun and day and night. Too common-place to unlock your doubting heart? Try imagining life without any one of them and then try thanking God again, one by one down the same list. The elder brother in the story of the prodigal son fell into the trap of ingratitude. He had always had his father and his father's house, but he could not share his father's heart. He was too ungrateful to permit himself to rejoice with his father when the prodigal brother came home at last. The father behaved in a way the elder son did not expect and so he doubted him; doubted his motives, doubted that the father loved *him* any longer because the old man gave a party to celebrate the homecoming of the wayward son.

Ingratitude leads to doubt and it also leads to taking for granted the common joys of life, which in turn leads to deeper doubt. The elder son, responsible and faithful though he had always been to his father, fell into the trap of having taken the good things of his father's house for granted. When we do this and, like the elder brother, experience shock at the Father's joy over a ne'er-do-well when at last he comes home, we begin to doubt the Father's love and our loyalty wavers. "What is my Father so excited about? How can he show this kind of special treatment to his no-good son who has wasted his gifts, when he does nothing special for me? He is giving no parties for me, and I am the one who has been with him and worked for him all these years his other son was away sinning. Why should this worthless brother cause so much joy in my Father's heart when I seem to cause none? Why doesn't he do something special for me too?" When we have been taking our goodnesses from God for granted, anyone can fall into this kind of doubt. When we take his gifts for granted, we begin to doubt the Giver.

Dr. Helmut Thielicke points out that the elder brother *dissociated* himself from his own brother, the prodigal son of the father. When he was registering his complaint to the father, he did not say, "My brother;" he called the boy "your son." It seems to me *dissociation* leads to doubt. When we lose sight of the wideness of God's love, we lose sight of God. When we reach the place of self-satisfaction where we cannot any longer conceive of

God's loving any other person as he loves us, we have lost sight of the quality of love that drew us in the first place. We then begin to doubt this "strange" God, who has (to us) grown less dynamic. It is really *we* who have shut ourselves off from the knowledge of the depth and the breadth of his love, but without knowing why, we find ourselves less attracted to him. When we lose the ability to rejoice with God over the return of the most repulsive, humanly worthless man, we have lost our contact with the heart of God. God has not lessened his love for us, but in the lessening of our love for him, in the shrinking of our capacity to share God's longing over everyone, we have fallen easy victims to doubt. Christians who dissociate themselves from their fellow Christians for whatever reason should be watchful: They could be slipping toward doubt.

A Christian leader once confided to me about a colleague: "I was so happy that this man had agreed to sit with me on the platform that night, that I embarrassed him, I think, by throwing my arms around him instead of shaking hands. It was an impulse on my part. I knew this man had crucified me in his writings and from his pulpit, but I somehow shared enough of the joy of God that my brother had chosen to appear with me that I embraced him without thinking. I pray I didn't humiliate him too much." A saintly, God-motivated impulse. Not consciously being "loving"—not meaning to appear noble, just acting (reacting) on a love impulse from

God. Doubt does not come easily to a man like that.
He did not call the critical brother "God's son"; he
called him " my brother."

We have said nothing about the so-called *scientific doubt* concerning the miracles and the stories
in the Bible. I do not feel qualified to write of this
kind of mind, except to say that I believe God *did*
"fashion all our hearts alike." Jesus' disciple
Thomas evidently had what we think of as an in-
quiring, scientific mind. But his doubts fled once
Jesus himself appeared before him and eased
Thomas' guilt by inviting him to feel the scars in
his hands and side. Thomas had apparently always
lived under a question mark, had always demanded
the why of everything, and Jesus put him at rest.
After all, God had created the mind of Thomas too.
He knew it demanded proof and so he gave it,
gladly, eagerly, making a special trip back to the
room where the disciples hid from the authorities
when he knew Thomas would be there. God is like
this. He not only knows us exactly as we are, no
effort required to reach us is ever too much trouble
for him. God knew, too, that the kind of doubt
Thomas had was genuine intellectual doubt, and
this is rather rare. Most of us doubt from another
source. We doubt from carelessness within our own
hearts, from willful sin, from ingratitude, from superiority, from selfishness—seldom truly from our
intellects.

The most common cause for doubt is, perhaps,

self-pity. When we sink into this most destructive of pits, we can't possibly think God is treating us "right" and so we fly to the refuge of doubt. Strange, isn't it, that so often those who have more reason from a human standpoint to be sorry for themselves, seldom are? Great tragedy and piled-up troubles can do one of two things to us: They can either drive us to God or into a pit of self-pity. If we permit our hardships to drive us to God, our pity increases, but it is directed then toward others who need us. If we tumble into the pit of self-sympathy, our pity increases also, but it is toward ourselves and eventually we smother in it. I have come to believe that self-pity and doubt are bed-fellows. One breeds the other. I also know that faith and self-pity cannot live together in the same human heart. One will snuff out the other.

God knows about our doubts, even the ones we have missed seeing. And they do not shock or surprise him. We are not told to get rid of them and *then* turn to God. As Jesus said, we are to bring our burdens, our heavy loads along with us when we come. And nothing is heavier than doubt.

7

Fightings and fears within, without, . . .

There is no indication anywhere that God expects our civil wars to end before we come to him. There is no indication that he expects us to stop being afraid before we accept his invitation. We are—all of us, every minute, *invited*—just as we are. And there isn't a human being among us who isn't fearful of something, who isn't defending himself against something or someone . . . fighting in some way to survive.

In fact, fear causes fighting and fighting causes fear. It seems to me increasingly evident that the

75

two are partners; devastating, tireless partners bent upon keeping us from the quality of relationship God intends us all to have with him and with each other.

"The entire atmosphere of our household is permeated by my daughter's fear. Since her husband was killed in Vietnam the child hasn't slept through a single night (and he was one of the early casualties.) It has been three years now, as I write this letter, and although some of her grief has diminished, her fear seems to increase. We have taken her to psychiatrists, she is on tranquilizers constantly, but nothing seems to help. I grieve for her, but I also grieve for her small child and for my husband and me."

This kind of fear becomes a sickness. One about which I personally know almost nothing. One about which I would not attempt to write. No one book can cover every aspect of every human twist and certainly only those who are trained should try. I am not trained, but this much seems evident from the remainder of the distraught mother's letter: The young woman did not know God *before* the tragedy occurred. By the mother's admission, no one in the family knows him now. We can only be realistic here, not critical. Most people do not know God personally! And few are as honest as this correspondent. I could only urge *her* to surrender her own life to him and go on from there. I do not know *how* he will do it; each situation is different—

some seem hopeless, but if God is God, there *is* a way through.

I have used this extreme, apparently hopeless, example at the outset to clarify for those who are experiencing similar agonies, that although nothing is impossible to God, patience is required and a realistic viewpoint. I am skeptical of the glib Christian who belittles the torment of excessive fear, who tosses off a Scripture verse, confident that if *he* were in the same spot, he would *not* doubt God. For almost five years now, I have heard occasionally from an intelligent, caring, deeply Christian mother whose daughter also is caught in abnormal fear patterns. We have not yet, any of us, found the key to God's plan for healing her. There are no glib, quick answers. There is the eternal fact of God and there is the potential of our faith.

And there is the continuing invitation from Jesus Christ.

We tend to drop the line from the old song into the slot labeled "fightings and fears of the *penitent*." God does urge the repentant person to come, bringing along his "fightings and fears within, without." Those of us who have come, dragging this heavy load, know he welcomes us this way—in this unsettled, restless condition of heart. But he also includes the believer who, although he has made the initial turning to Christ, still finds himself doing battle—"within, without"—with his fears. New circumstances enter our lives—sudden death,

illness, financial crises, old age, devastating loss—
and even though we haven't been abnormally
afraid for years because of our faith in God's involvement with us, we are, one day or one high
noon or one night, afraid again. And, because fighting does accompany fear, we are, after all those
years of peace, in the thick of the battle again.

What of us?

First of all, we will almost inevitably add to our
fightings by jumping into a cloak of false guilt.
Haven't we known years of peace with God? Haven't
we lived more or less adequate, useful lives without
the debilitating signs of fear? Haven't we believed
that our faith has been in the God who does not,
who cannot change? Why, if our faith has really
been in God himself, and not merely in our Christian fellowship or isolated texts or good works, are
we now suddenly afraid?

Of course, this can be a most important time of
discovery for us. Many, many persons find out
when trouble comes that their faith has not been in
God. That it has been in some aspect of God's service or in some particular gift. I believe there are
perhaps millions of Christians whose faith is really
in their own salvation. We tend to love God because he saved *us*. We tend to trust him because he
saved *us*, not because he *is* the Saviour. Here is a
danger, as I see it, of thinking of one's faith as
being in the blood of Christ. The blood has been
shed, once and for all. His *life*, his *being* go on.

And we can go on unaware through year after year, that we have placed our confidence in almost anything else but the Lord himself—until some crisis occurs which chokes us with fear and causes us to fight both the crisis and God.

At this point, *if* we have learned to look at life from the viewpoint of God and not from the perspective of our own feelings, we can rejoice. We can rejoice because anyone at any time in his life can begin to trust God alone. Not the church, not the Bible, not baptism, not holy communion, not spiritual "experience," not salvation, not soul-winning— God.

To place one's faith in any *part* of Christianity is as useless as placing one's faith in the wings, the engines, the landing gear, the radar equipment of an airplane. The entire plane is required for flight. No part will be adequate alone. The authentic Christian life which can cope with fear and conflict is the life which is dependent upon the person of Jesus Christ alone. He himself *is* Christianity.

And so, if we find we have been trusting one of the forms of our faith and not God, the fear that brought us to this insight can be the greatest blessing of all.

We can then shed our cloak of false guilt and give thanks for our fear. You see, if we have, for example, placed our faith in a verse of Scripture about fear intended only to enlighten, false guilt is inevitable. "Perfect love casts out fear" is one of the

79

most enlightening lines in the entire Bible but, misunderstood or superficially interpreted, it can cause
an enormous amount of false guilt. We either tend
to think the "perfect love" refers to our love
(which can never be perfect in this life) or we
somehow feel we are not "advanced" enough to let
God's perfect love cast out our fear. Neither of
these could possibly be what God intended us to get
from this verse. Surely, he meant for it to do the
one thing necessary: to drive us to a still deeper understanding of his nature. God's perfect love does
not cast out our fear according to how "advanced"
we are spiritually. This limits God. This takes the
measure of the power of his redeeming love by our
understanding of it! The Word of God here is in-
structing us to remember that when we are united
to Christ, who *is* perfect love, we will find out for
ourselves that there is no ground where fear can
take permanent root. We will all always know flash
fears—sudden bad news, the missing plane, the over-
drawn checking account, the telephone call that
comes too late—all of these will make us afraid, but
our fear will not take permanent, destructive root
within us if we have learned that God is depend-
able.*

If our faith has been in the Scripture above the
Person of God, sudden tragedy can cut us off from
words. If our faith has been in the safe-seeming,

* I explored this idea in *The Wider Place* (Grand Rapids:
Zondervan, 1966).

cozy world of our own church, the doors may be closed and the lights out when our tragedy strikes. The church and the Bible are sources of knowledge about God. They are the places we turn for help in building faith. But our faith must be actively in the living Christ before his perfect love can cast out our fear. Can hold us steady when we would fight against what may happen to us.

I grow afraid, just as you do. But my fear, even of the death of a loved one (most difficult of all for me), lives and grows only as long as I turn to other people with it; only as long as I try to overcome it myself. It is cast out (the unhealthy, destructive fear—not the circumstance) when I deliberately remember Jesus. There are, of course, times for us all when the fear is too sharp, the shock too sudden for us deliberately to do anything. God knows this. And I believe this is why he worked things out as he did, so that our only peace is in *him*. No one is ever forgotten by Christ and there is no such thing as his being away from us. We can turn our attention from him, but never, for one minute, does he turn his attention from us.

I was on a speaking engagement at a university campus when the telephone call came from my brother telling me that my father had acute leukemia. In ten minutes I was due at a professor's house for lunch. My first impulse was to beg off. I could think of only one thing: If I can get by myself with God, then I won't be so afraid my dad is going to die. To cancel seemed out of the question. The luncheon was in my honor. I went. Quite naturally, I sought the comfort of the Christian people there. They tried. I didn't really hear them. They over-tried at first and then they worked at getting my mind off it. This, of course, was utterly futile. I tried to eat to be polite, but then the old fear would almost choke me. In a few minutes, I didn't seem to hear their talk any more; I could swallow again and, as though we were sitting at that table alone, God took over for me. It was no time to hunt feverishly for a Scripture; I was attending a lunch-eon with comparative strangers. I was not in a church—my salvation didn't occur to me as such, but God was there in person, and *he* cast out my paralyzing fear. Of course, I rushed home to my father's bedside as fast as I could get away, but in all the long months that followed while the dread-ful disease was killing him, the first panic, the first helpless fear did not return once. The more I was with my father during those last weeks, the more I loved him, the more I longed to keep him with me; but there was no fear.

God does not promise to wipe out the reason for our fear. He promises by his very nature, to wipe out the fear.

Some of us are more fearful by nature than oth-ers. This we need to recognize. It can keep some of the more naturally courageous among us spiritually humble. But again, God's action in behalf of our fears is in no way dependent upon our nature. It is entirely dependent upon his nature, and his nature *is* perfect love. It is natural to God to rush to our side when we need him. It is natural to God to become immediately involved—more accurately, it is natural to God to *stay* totally involved with all that concerns his loved ones. And if only we could remember that we are *not* his loved ones because we are good or obedient or deserving, we would find resting in his love far simpler. Like the father of the prodigal, our Father experiences only gladness when any of us, for any reason, rushes to him for help.

What of our little, nagging fears? Somehow it is easier to remember that God is there when the big fears strike and our friends sympathize than when the little ones stay around day after day, almost unnoticed by anyone but us. Little barnacle fears that don't show because they are submerged beneath the image we want to present to the world. Fear of not being wanted, of having been invited out of pity or duty. Fear of our family's using us as a convenience, not appreciating us. Fear of speaking in public, of praying aloud with our friends. Fear of the dentist, of what the doctor will say. Fear of meeting new people, of losing our jobs. Fear of growing old, of a long, lingering illness. Fear of the money running out. Fear of the unknown.

In these areas we have the most flagrant examples of fears which cause us to fight. If we fear what the doctor will say, we fight anyone who tries to get us to make an appointment. If we fear losing our jobs, we can begin to fight our fellow workers who seem safe in theirs. If we fear growing old, we fight to prove we are still young, or fight those around us because we don't know what else to do with the fear inside. Entire families have been thrown into chaos and conflict because one member feared his or her money would run out. Fears mark us, twist our personalities, make life miserable for those unfortunate enough to know us.

But the same answer applies: God. In the first place, only God knows these hidden fears thoroughly. We are so loath to admit them even to ourselves that we try to call them by other names. But he knows exactly what they are and what caused them. If a man becomes eaten up with the hidden fear of losing his job, he is (however unconsciously) simply not trusting the Father to take care of his needs as Jesus said he would. He is saying in effect, that Jesus did not really mean what he said about the lilies of the field. If a woman fears growing old so that her personality is warped by it, she is saying in effect that God's goodness and mercy will *not* follow her all the days of her life. He did not promise happiness or prosperity or long life, but he did promise to be with us: "Lo, I am with you always." And if our faith is in him alone, this brings peace, because "he is our peace."

Jesus seemed always aware of the fears of his disciples. "Fear not," he said, "it is I." Do we dare believe that God is *in* everything that makes us afraid? Not that he sends the things that frighten us, but that he is *in* them with us?

A young boy who feared storms abnormally began repeating Jesus' words every time the thunder began to roll: "Be not afraid, it is I." His fear came under control.

A close friend, while reading a manuscript of mine was freed of a new, painful fear when she came upon the same words: "Be not afraid, it is I." She had been treated with extreme cruelty by an official of a Christian organization—forced to resign suddenly after many years of service. Now, she did not begin to believe that Jesus Christ had caused this Christian brother to deal her this blow. She knew God too well for that. But the fact that Christ *recognized* and *understood* that the injustice had made her more afraid than hurt reminded her in the midst of her shock that God was there in it all, and she knew peace.

Perfect love does cast out fear, but it is not done by some remote, authoritarian act of God. He, himself, *is* this perfect love and after we are honest enough to recognize our fears for what they are, we need do only one thing: Come to him, bringing the fears and the fightings with us.

Some instances of fear are beyond us to understand. Surely, God's way of handling our fears is beyond us. There must be no settling for the glib answer. But it is not glib to contend that "with God all things are possible." After all, this is nothing one of us thought up. Jesus said it first.

8

Just as I am—poor, wretched, blind; . . .

When I am weak, then can I become strong. When I am poor, then am I in a position to become rich. The great paradox of the Gospel goes on. And those who have grasped its meaning know God. Those who have learned to look through the right end of the glass go forward. Those who continue to attempt to understand life from the vantage-point of man fail—continue to be tossed about by their conflicts and doubts, their fightings and fears.

Jesus said: "Blessed are the poor in spirit: for theirs is the kingdom of heaven." What did he mean? In Luke's version the words "in spirit" were omitted. When we consider Jesus' statement as reading: "Blessed be ye poor for yours is the kingdom of heaven," we can become easily confused. It is difficult for us to imagine finding blessedness in material poverty. But, happily, the words used by Matthew: "poor *in spirit*" have turned up in the Dead Sea Scrolls, so there seems to be no more need for confusion. Since there is nothing blessed or ethical about involuntary poverty, Jesus was obviously speaking of those in spiritual need. More accurately, those who have come to *see* their spiritual need. Often in the Psalms "poor" is used to describe those who, out of their conscious need, have cast themselves on God. The "poor" to whom the Servant of the Lord was anointed to preach the good news.

Now, none of this has to do with the overly submissive, weak-spined person. Jesus did not say, "Blessed are the *poor spirited*." He said, "Blessed are the poor *in* spirit." Blessed, then—happy, indeed, is the man who has come to see the tremendous potential of dependence upon God; the economy of energy and the rest involved in not trying to carry the load himself. Blessed is the man who has discovered the creativity of accepting joy from God and no longer fighting for happiness on his own.

Jesus used the same logic throughout the Beatitudes. If we grasp his meaning in one, we have them all. Just as he declared that those who hunger shall be filled, so he declared that those who have recognized their poverty of spirit, shall be made rich by receiving the kingdom of heaven itself. The man who is pure in heart—single-minded, intent first of all upon God—shall come to know him as he is. A man cannot be pure in heart, intent upon God, until he has come to see his own spiritual poverty. Cannot be filled until he hungers.

So much has been written on the meaning of the Beatitudes; it seems a mystery why so many of us go on concocting our own descriptions, our own concepts of what the genuinely Christian life is like. In the Beatitudes, the Master himself is telling us concisely, clearly. And yet we go right on being depressed, disturbed, rushing to counselors and books and retreats because our spiritual poverty *must* mean that something is terribly wrong! When we feel poor in spirit, things are never more right. Jesus says this is the healthy state of a human heart eager for God.

It seems to me we couldn't be further off balance than when we become agitated at our own poverty of spirit. We act in a way we know is wrong, selfish, unkind, and off we go for human help. What we are really declaring is that we thought we were much more stable, self-sufficient Christians— incapable of doing a thing like this or that. Our pride is wounded and instead of recognizing our healthy need of God, we collapse. Instead of receiving more light, we hide what we have under a bushel. Jesus said that if we are poor in spirit the kingdom of heaven belongs to us! If we own the kingdom of heaven by merely leaning on God instead of our pious selves, why do we go down under the discovery of our spiritual poverty—the very qualification he insists we need?

You, *just as you are,* equal total need of God. I *just as I am,* equal total need of God. When, consciously or unconsciously, we have tried to barge ahead of God and have shocked ourselves by our lack of spirituality we can admit it and rejoice. There is then, of all times, no need to despair. *Blessed* are we then, because, according to Jesus, the kingdom of heaven belongs to us. We have access to all that God offers when we stop trying to decorate his gifts with our own talents. We have access to the energy of God when we stop trying to overassist him.

None of this belittles us. Jesus was not trying to make us feel inferior. He was simply clarifying the way things really are. We are we and God is God. God needs us to be with him, but we need him to be *in* us. Our spirits are *poor* alone. But in union with his spirit, life begins. Our spirits are incomplete alone. In union with the Spirit of God, we are complete. "Ye are complete in him." We find that the kingdom of heaven *is* at hand.

It is a mistake to attempt to pick ourselves up with pep pills and the company of other people who think us rich in spirit. It is a mistake, it is a waste, and it is in direct opposition to what God tells us to do.

A clergyman grew confidential with me once: "Do you know how I think a lot of us ministers get by our own rough times? I can speak for myself, at least. I hurry to a service or make a house call on some depressed parishioner. I go, it seems to me, almost any place to avoid going to God in my poverty of spirit. It's simpler to seek out other human beings who think I'm spiritually sturdy. It's easier to turn on my platform manner at a service and imagine my spirituality intact, than it is to go to God."

A man as honest as that did not stay spiritually poor for long, I'm certain. In fact, I felt that he was "going to God" even as he was being honest with me.

We do not need to perform any certain act, carry out any ritual. God *rushes* to cooperate with the person who recognizes his own spiritual poverty. If we could only reach the simplicity of Brother Lawrence, the saintly monastery cook, who turned to the Lord each time he saw himself in need and said: "You see, Lord, this is the way I am without you."

This is absolutely all that is required. We are to come, just as we are, bringing our needy spirits.

According to the dictionary, the word "wretched" means: *Deeply afflicted, dejected, or distressed. Very miserable.*

It also means: *Hatefully contemptible; despica-*

ble. Very poor in quality or ability; mean, unsatis-factory, worthless.

This would seem to cover the wretchedness of most of us. When I first began to study the lyrics of "Just As I Am," I rather questioned the use of the word "wretched" and wondered if it had any archaic meaning with which we are not familiar. Not that I doubt our wretchedness for a minute. But in the next line of this stanza, when the author writes of God's action on our wretchedness, she writes: "healing of the mind."

When "Just As I Am" was composed in the nine-teenth century, people weren't conditioned to psy-chiatry as we are now. And I often wonder if we aren't missing a great deal from God by thinking only of those pronounced mentally ill when we think of the need for the Father to heal a mind.

Is it possible that many of us need healing of our minds, although we are not ill mentally according to psychiatric diagnosis? Could we look at ourselves for a moment in the light of the ordinary dictionary definition of the word "wretched"?

Deeply afflicted. Is anyone excluded here? There is almost no one past his childhood who, in some way, has never been deeply afflicted. We are af-flicted by illness, by the illness of our loved ones, by grief, by fear, by frustration, by jealousy, by self-ishness, by the tendency to worry, to be anxious. We are afflicted by pride and stubbornness and the chaos that follows sudden tragedy. Life afflicts us. Jesus said it would. "In this world ye shall *have* tribulation." His is not a butterfly religion. He is not a stargazer and he does not expect us to be. In fact, he warns us about it. We are never sent off by Christ to live our lives gazing at stars or chasing butterflies. He knew life would afflict us. He permitted it to afflict him, so that we would know that he knows. Jesus allowed wretchedness in his own heart, so we would feel free to bring our wretchedness to him for healing. Anything that afflicts us in any way—disturbs our minds, distorts our thinking—causes us to misdirect our thoughts.

Do we not need healing of our minds when we are deeply afflicted?

Do we not need healing of our minds when we are *dejected* or *distressed?* When we are *very miserable?* Doesn't dejection over any situation disturb our ability to think clearly? Can you read a profound book when you are "worried half to death" over something? Even if you are musically trained, can you follow the intricate patterns of a Bach Fugue when you are distressed? Is your mind capable of clear concentration in times of dejection and distress? Mine isn't. And during those times I need healing of my mind. During those times when you are *very miserable,* you, too, need healing of your mind. Our minds control our emotions and set our wills in action. When our minds are confused, tormented, depressed, our emotions run wild and our wills are without reins. We are *wretched,* and we need healing.

Now, we can all experience affliction, dejection, distress—misery, from causes outside our control. But how about the second set of dictionary definitions for the word "wretched": *hatefully contemptible; despicable; very poor in quality or ability; mean, unsatisfactory, worthless. . .*

Does it appear that these traits might spring *from* us? That our wretchedness, as a consequence of our own contemptible spirits, our own unsatisfactory attitudes, our own worthlessness, can fall under the classification of our lack of responsibility of life? To God?

This meaning of the word throws the responsibility firmly upon us and we see that we must act if our wretchedness is to diminish. True, our feeling of wretchedness will be more acute if our troubles stem from our own lack to effort, our own lack of stability, but God's invitation covers this too. Covers us—just as we are: *hatefully contemptible, despicable, very poor in quality or ability, mean, unsatisfactory, worthless.*

It is undoubtedly simpler for a person to come to God if he knows he has caused his own wretchedness. When we know we are responsible for our trouble, it isn't so difficult to see our need for healing. The person wretched from some affliction over which he has no control may more quickly sink into self-pity. Somehow it doesn't occur to us that our minds need healing just because life has knocked us down, but they do. And, the invitation is all-inclusive from God. "He will heal their afflictions. . . ."

Just as I am, poor, wretched—*blind*. We all have blind spots. Only one Man ever walked the earth with total spiritual sight. Realizing this has been almost like having my sight restored after the darkness. If we can learn to see the blind spots in our brothers as inability *to see* in certain areas, we can forgive more easily. There is no excuse for any of us to remain blind when we are in union with the Healer, but we do. I find it simpler to be kind than I once did, when a brother acts in a way that makes me want to cut him down to size—*if* I realize he may still be blind spiritually.

If we have picked up our crosses to follow Christ in love, we will try not to be blind to the blindness of others. It is quite true that a person may be stubborn and not blind at all on a certain point. But it still seems the safest thing for us to assume, at least, that he is blind. He could be, you know. And only remorse could follow our kicking a blind man who has unknowingly bumped into us.

One of my dearest friends in Chicago, aged ninety, was in the hospital for two months in intense pain. She didn't proclaim her Christianity from the housetops. She just lived it and cheered us with her sense of humor and her courage through the long hours as we watched her suffer. After every cringe of pain, she smiled and winked at one of us, making very certain that we didn't worry too much. One day she will go to heaven and no one there will feel more at home in the midst of the rejoicing and the dancing.

My elderly friend had a roommate at the hospital who tried our souls as much as my friend blessed us. The roommate, who weighed at least two hundred and fifty pounds, had only a minor injury to one arm. But with her good hand, she clutched her Bible and forced anyone and everyone to listen as she read aloud chapter after chapter. Whether we felt like praying or not (and with my friend, we mostly felt like hugging and laughing), we had to pray when the notion struck the hefty roommate. She regaled us with the blessings of God upon her fine Christian service. "I never permit a day to go by without witnessing." And so on and on and on. But between every line of Scripture, she interpolated a pitiable groan. The doctor insisted she was no longer in pain. When her minister ducked almost furtively into the room to inquire how she felt, she invariably sighed and moaned: "Oh, just fair." The nurses on the floor, who used to make reasons for dropping by to see my cheerful old friend, began to avoid the room because the mournful, self-pitying, obese "saint" was there. They knew she would complain about something. This was par for her course. And so they didn't come in as often and my friend missed them.

The pious roommate was simply and tragically *blind*. I cannot believe that any normal human being would make such a fool of herself otherwise. At least an attempt to pity her blindness where the authentic Christian life is concerned helped me contain myself. We didn't enjoy it, but we tried to help her tie her robe, reach her glass of water, find her place in her Bible.

Not only was she blind to her own ridiculous religiosity, she was blind to God's nature too. Her almost total involvement in herself was the exact opposite of what we see when we look at the God she thought she followed. To her, *she* is the center of *God's* world. At the center of my elderly friend's world *is God*. These two follow opposite Gods and they are opposites to each other in every way.

One is blind; the other not only sees beyond human sight, she gives light.

The more I think on it, the more I am convinced that our spiritual blindness is directly due to our failure to see God as he is. If we are afraid to surrender ourselves to God for fear of what terrible thing he might ask us to do, we are at least partially blind to his nature. If we believe he punishes in any other way but the way of love, then we are blind to his heart. If we think there is some trick, some particular performance on our part which must be practiced with a certain kind of skill in order to live close to Jesus Christ, we are totally blind to his shepherd heart.

But he has told us to bring our blindness and come. To bring our blindness and our poverty of spirit and our wretchedness to him, so that he can heal us.

He *cannot* heal us until we do.

9

Sight, riches, healing of the mind,
Yea, all I need, in Thee to find, . . .

We all need clearer sight, we all need spiritual en-
richment, we all need healing of our minds.

If we do not know this, we have missed the key to
receiving from God. In missing this key, we have
not only missed his best for ourselves, we have
thwarted God. We have left him standing with his
gift-laden hands stretched toward us. We have
made our shameful addition to the picture of man
rushing to and fro before the Giver, as though he
were not there. More shameful is the fact that as we
rush back and forth before him, we are pleading

over our shoulders as we go, for the very things he has been offering all along: "Sight, riches, healing of the mind."

We give lip service to our needs—somehow it has a humble sound, but we don't begin, any of us, to take what he is constantly offering. Could it be that we honestly do not discern the fine line of difference between something we need and something we want? This could be. Only God knows in certain hairline situations. We may go into debt over our heads and as far as our creditors and our good names are concerned among men, we *need* God to send us some extra cash. But God knows there is a lesson here which we need more than we need the financial help. He stands holding out the lesson as we go rushing by pleading for money. The solution? Simply trust in his superior knowledge of things as they are.

Our receiving from God is directly related to his giving: He will not give us something that will in any way harm or weaken or spoil us. Not because he is strict, but because he is wise, and cares more about *us* than about our *desires*.

Old stuff, you say? Yes, it is. As old as from the beginning to now. God refused the man and woman in the garden the fruit of one tree. He refused it because he knew what would happen to them if they ate it. Death would happen, separation from his presence, utter loneliness for them, pain; and no more pleasures or necessities without hard work. He had already *given* them everything they needed and more. Perhaps he had not given them the "more" because, I firmly believe, joy and pleasure and laughter of the Eden variety are *necessities* to all people. God proved this by all he gave them from the beginning of their earthly lives. He did *not* give them what would harm them. There is no reason to think he would change his mind at this late date. All this is very old stuff, but the fact remains that we have not yet learned it. We go on confusing the issue, demanding from God what he cannot, in sensitive, steady love, give us.

And so, the question is never God's willingness to give the "riches" he knows we desperately need; the question is always our willingness to receive. Refuse a gift prepared for us by the Father? Indeed, yes. Every day of our lives. Sometimes many times a day, and our inability or refusal to recognize our need is at the bottom of our poverty. "He *will* fill the hungry with good things," but we don't know we are hungry. Or, if we know it, we are too proud to admit it even to the God who is already aware of it. We sing, "I need thee every hour . . ." and act another way. He offers joy—the pure joy of heaven, right here on earth. We walk past him, ignoring it because we have found what we stupidly call joy in things; in a safe, select circle of friends; in a successful career; in our families.

When God gives a thing, it is permanent. The joy of God is so sturdy, so enduring, so indestructible, nothing that can ever happen to us can diminish it. It may or may not have anything to do with laughter or happiness, but it always had to do with him, and therefore it is as unchangeable as the Lord God himself. God's gifts never wear out, but we are accustomed to wanting things that fall apart so we can then have the stimulation of buying new ones. The difference here is that with God's gifts there is no chance of boredom. The average American is so in the habit of buying a new car every two years that those of us who grow attached to an old one and keep it are thought eccentric. We buy new things, seek out new romances, new jobs, discard old friends for new ones, build new houses and buy new automobiles because basically we are bored. This is not always our reason, but too often it is, and I wonder if our boredom isn't an insult to God. Every day spent in simple, childlike trust in the Father can be a new beginning. At least he offers us a new beginning each time the sun comes up, but too often we are once more caught running back and forth ignoring his offer—bored.

God offers us sight, sight, sight. We prefer our blindness. He is trying every minute to get our attention, but we are running the other way, busy, perhaps, about his work, but still paying no attention to him.

I once experienced terror within my own being just from listening to a friend tell me of her first panic when, after an automobile accident, she knew she was permanently blinded. "I kept trying to wake up. I grabbed my eyes and tried to force my eyelids open. They were already open and I was looking as hard as I could look and it was still dark! Then they told me. For what seemed forever, I lay there trying to take it in and then it rushed in like a tidal wave—the terrible, helpless realization that I would never see my husband's face again—never see my children grow up. Never see the sky, the rain on a windowpane—all sorts of funny, daily things were suddenly so dear to me, I found myself clawing the air trying to get them all back! The trap was everywhere and the darkness filled me with such terror, I thought if I didn't get out of it, I would die. I reached for the wall beside my bed and beat it as hard as I could, first with my fists and then with my head. Finally, when they subdued me, I cried until I was exhausted. And for days, I grabbed. Every time my husband bent over me, I grabbed his dear head in my hands, and felt it all over as though my hands could help me see him. I kept pressing his forehead against first one sightless eye and then the other." She smiled. "My grabbing included my children too and I frightened them terribly. Their fear helped me begin to accept it, I suppose, more than anything else. But as long as I felt so trapped, I wanted to grab all that mattered to me and hold on for dear life."

As long as I felt so trapped, I wanted to grab all that mattered to me and hold on for dear life.

God is always offering freedom to us, but we are trapped in our blindness, and so we grab. I will never forget my friend's use of the word "trapped." There must be no panic like the panic that comes with the sudden loss of our physical eyesight. The trap must seem complete during those first hours of unnatural, new darkness. And as I write these lines, for the first time there comes to me the thought: What would the terror be like if, once we had been given gift of spiritual sight, we lost it! The entrapment would be more than we could bear. The darkness more dense than the once-lighted human heart could endure. The panic would be complete. But the God who gives never takes his gifts away. Once he has given us new life, new sight is ours forever. We can stop using it, but the spiritual sight which comes from God cannot be lost as physical sight can be lost.

The horror of losing one's physical eyesight as an adult is, of course, more acute than blindness from birth. If we have never seen a sunset, we don't miss it in the same way in which those who have seen it do. If we have "seen" our loved ones' faces only with our hands and our spiritual sight, we do not panic at the darkness quite as much. At least, so I have been told by those who have been blind from birth. And this is, perhaps, some of the way it is for us who have lived in spiritual darkness, outside the knowledge of Christ, until we were adults. The darkness was there, but never having seen the light, we did not fight our darkness as we would fight it now, should God's light suddenly go out.

More nonbelievers would come to Christ if we, who dwell in his light, acted as though we could see. If we acted as though our darkness had been filled with the very light of the presence of the one who called himself "the light of the world." There could be no better way to spread the good news Christ came bringing from the Father, but we go on trying every other conceivable way and we go on with little notable success. A woman wrote: "I have talked until I am blue in the face, trying to win my son-in-law to Christ. He just laughs at me and says he hasn't seen a thing in any church member that convinced him *they* had any better God than he has."

We *talk* about our sight and refuse to see into the darkness of the lives around us. Or if we see, we refuse to act on our sight. This young man did not need *talk*—he needed understanding. The kind that comes from seeing from the viewpoint of God.

We Christians *see* the needs of our world; we see and we write checks and we talk. But this is only partial obedience to the law of light, to the law of continuing sight from God. Jesus restored sight to the man blind from his birth, but he involved the man in the healing too. "A man that is called Jesus made clay, and anointed mine eyes, and said unto me, Go to the pool of Siloam, and wash: and I went and washed, and I received sight." Jesus always does his part. We do not always do ours. This man *went* to the pool as he was instructed, and washed. When, after Saul had been blinded by the sight of Christ on the road to Damascus, the Lord sent his servant Ananias to heal Saul's eyes, Saul was told to *receive*. We cannot know all that this involved for Saul, the persecutor of Christians, but Ananias said, "Brother Saul, *receive* thy sight." Perhaps Saul's new Lord had made it clear in the temporary darkness that Saul, the persecutor, would become Paul, the bond-slave of Jesus Christ; would be given heavy responsibility for his restored sight, would be commissioned to make use of it even unto death. At any rate, God did not restore Saul's sight willynilly. Saul was told to *receive* it.

God restores our sight, keeps it sharp, according to our cooperation with him. He wastes nothing. He will give us sight as we are willing to use it; willing to act upon what we see.

God does not give foolishness; he gives *riches*. ". . . the mouth of fools feedeth on foolishness." God feeds his people with the nourishment that will "lift them up forever." This is the God who "fed them according to the *integrity* of his heart." If this one line could become reality for us, we *could* have no more poverty of spirit. Perhaps God's integrity is dim for us because we have, in our century, seemed almost to drop the word "integrity" from our vocabularies. We center on success, quantity, increased production, crowds, "out-reach." But the man or woman fed according to the integrity of God's own heart could never be poor-spirited, could never be hungry for the destructive food of fools. "He will fill the hungry with *good* things"— according to the *integrity* of the One who created the capacity for hunger into our beings. The adequate Christian goes on hungering for more and more of God. "As the hart panteth after the waterbrooks, so panteth my soul for thee, O God." The healthy Christian is the man or woman who never discovers on this earth all he or she wants of God. But this kind of hunger breeds unsatisfaction, never dissatisfaction. God never surfeits us with anything. "He shall feed his flock like a shepherd." The shepherd knows the capacity of his sheep. And he also knows their limitations. "I will feed my flock, and I will cause them to lie down, saith the Lord God." He is balanced. God is not prodding the frantic Christian who exhausts both himself and his friends by seeking more and more of a "Christian experience." He will feed us, but he will also cause us to lie down and stop eating when we need to rest. "I am frantic," a woman once said to me, "because it has been over a month now since I've had an elevating experience with God!" She was frantic and she was also foolish. God gives us mountaintop moments with him when he knows we need them. But his preception is perfect. This woman had come to depend upon her experience of exhilaration and not upon God. He feeds us balanced meals: meat and salad, as well as dessert.

". . . I will set up one shepherd over them, and he shall feed them . . . ; he shall feed them, and he shall be their shepherd."

The Shepherd has come. The balanced, sensitive-hearted, gracious Son of God is here to feed us and to see that we rest, so that our food can strengthen us for love.

". . . they shall feed and lie down, and none shall make them afraid." The same Shepherd who supplies the "riches" supplies the rest: *the healing of our minds*. "For the Lamb which is in the midst of the throne shall feed them, and shall lead them unto living fountains of waters; and God shall wipe away all tears from their eyes."

Is this kind of peace of mind possible for the children of God only in heaven? I believe with all my heart, it is for us now. Our capacities for peace will increase once we are no longer pinned to earth by our mortal bodies, just as our capacities for joy will increase. But Jesus said he came *to this earth*, so we "might have life, and have it more abundantly." He did not limit this offer to the next life. He spoke to the condition of men standing before him in the crowds that followed him along the dusty roads of Galilee and Judea. He went about the countryside and up and down the city streets, healing those with sick and troubled minds as well as those with crippled bodies and blind eyes. Jesus cast seven devils out of the mind of Mary Magdalene, and restored her to such sanity and balance that she was the one he could trust to see him first the morning he walked out of his tomb!

Worry is perhaps the most flagrant disturber of our minds. A physician once told me that a man *can* actually worry himself to death. We now know that an alarming amount of illness is caused by our disturbed minds, our twisted emotions. "I'm worried sick" is an apt diagnosis for much of our illness in the twentieth century. It had been true for centuries before ours, but now we have discovered something, at least, of the tremendous effects our minds have over our bodies. The mental-discipline cults *do* effect "healings" because they teach control of the mind. But for most of us, when worry comes, it is only added to if we have to work on discipline too. Discipline is essential, but discipline of the mind that is under the control of Christ is doubly effective. Children stop crying and lose their fears when their father comes on the scene, if he is a good father, because he is, in a sense, in control of their young lives. They are *his* responsibility. It is up to him to take care of them, to keep them from harm.

When a frightened child stops crying in his father's arms, his troubled mind has been healed.

The healing of our minds does not come from

some overt, outside-in act of God. It comes from union with God. It comes from an awareness of his presence within us in the midst of our turmoil. His presence, welcomed by us, in our personal lives. Healing comes from consciousness of his love, the kind of certainty that causes our faith to act involuntarily. If we know a person is trustworthy, if we *know* we are loved, we automatically trust that person. No struggle is required. No expectation to whip up. We *expect* from God *if* we know him.

It must be remembered here that at the outset it was (I hope) made clear that this book is being written to persons with reasonably normal minds. We are the only ones to whom I have any authority to write. We are the ones who are *apt not* to face our need for the healing of our minds, because we know we are not psychotic.

Many of us don't act like it, but most of us would admit that God is able to heal our minds. More than that, those of us who know him in any authentic way, know of his unwavering willingness to heal us. And yet we go on being nervous, high-strung, domineering, critical, anxious, insecure, worried. Why is this?

I don't know all the reasons, but a few are evident. The first one we have covered: We don't face our need for mental healing from God. We feel pretty much like everyone else, so we just don't think of turning to God to heal our confusions, our stubbornnesses, our bad tempers, our critical natures, our impatience.

There are also some who are faithful in their church lives, but who have not yet discovered the potential of a personal relationship with Jesus Christ. Have never experienced the creative habit of including him in all the daily, mundane, seemingly trivial problems. As a result, they operate their personal lives on moral principles alone, making tiring efforts to live up to what is considered "the good life." They need healing from their wearing self-effort.

But some of us who know him, who have experienced a personal relationship with him, are deliberately blocking his healing because we have failed to obey him on one point or another. Old stuff, also? Yes. Ancient. And one example of headstrong disobedience which blocks healing of our minds should be enough to make the point. We are specifically told in the Old Testament to make restitution where restitution is required. "If fire break out, and catch in thorns, so that the stacks of corn, or the standing corn, or the field, be consumed therewith; he that kindled the fire shall surely make restitution." And again, "If a man shall cause a field or vineyard to be eaten, and shall put in his beast, and shall feed in another man's field; of the best of his own field, and of the best of his own vineyard, shall he make restitution." In no way did

Christ detract from this, or make the law of restitution of no effect. We do not have to *earn* our salvation; it is a free gift from God and it comes at once when we place our faith in his Son, Jesus Christ. But those of us who have done this can testify quickly that almost at once—as out of nowhere—comes the compulsion to make restitution for the wrongs we have done. Not only to repay or make amends for any material wrongdoing—cheating, outright stealing, borrowing without returning—but to ask forgiveness for the heartbreak we have caused, the reputations we have damaged. It seems almost out of style, spiritually, to mention these things, but they block the healing of our minds. God is neither old nor new fashioned. He has always been and will always be *contemporary*. "One day is with the Lord as a thousand years, and a thousand years as one day." Whether it is currently "in" to make restitution is beside the point with God. He is eternal, unchanging; and this is a basic law of his, laid down for our spiritual healing.

When Jacob was an old man, he spoke of "the God which fed me all my life long unto this day." We can speak of God, too, at the close of our earthly lives, as Jacob did, if we have remained open to receive from him our sight, our riches, and the healing of our minds.

We cannot receive God in honesty without receiving his gifts. They are never separate from the

Giver. He does not portion out a bit of this and a lot of that, withholding himself. "All I need, in *Thee* to find, O Lamb of God, I come, I come!"

And no one has ever come and found him "away."

10

Just as I am, Thou wilt receive,
Wilt welcome, pardon, cleanse, relieve; . . .

To be welcomed means that we have been received gladly into someone's presence. We are willingly admitted, invited to enter, to stay, to enjoy, to accept hospitality.

Is this the way God welcomes us? Dare we come as we are with God? Could it possibly be true that we need not bring a gift? That we need not wear our finest garments? That we need not be wise or learned or even moral?

There is no other way to come into the presence of God if we are realistic. If we boned up and were

115

wise, he would know it was for effect. If we wore our best clothes, he would see through our effort to impress him. If we brought a gift, he would know we were attempting to obligate him. I speak now of our initial entrance into life with Christ. The welcome of God is a wholehearted welcome to us—*as we are*. He welcomes our gifts too, but they are meaningless until we have given ourselves to him. He never scorns our puny efforts to guarantee a welcome; he simply sees them as irrelevant. And he waits for us to bring ourselves.

One of the meanings of the word "receive" is "to have capacity for." God alone has the capacity to receive us—as we are. "I just can't believe God would accept me until I find the courage to stop this thing I'm doing. No matter how often I'm told that he *is* willing, I still can't believe it. What would God want with me?"

What would God want with me?

One thing: God wants to love us freely. When he is kept at arm's length, his love is there, but we refuse it. I doubt that anyone has ever understood what God's love causes Him to do. I doubt that anyone will ever understand what God's love causes Him to be. But anyone can experience that love, because everyone is welcome to his heart—*without one plea*.

The alcoholic on Skid Row is as welcome as the cultivated churchwoman. And the cultivated churchwoman is as welcome as the alcoholic on

Skid Row. The self-righteous religionist is as welcome to enter into the presence of the God of the universe as the prostitute. The prostitute is as welcome to enter into the presence of God as the self-righteous religionist. It is, of course, easier for the alcoholic on Skid Row and the prostitute to come—to bring themselves. Their adoration may come alive more quickly because they don't feel they have brought God much. But all are welcome—*just as they are*.

There is, after all, no way for us to be other than just as we are *until* we have come to God. This is what is so difficult for us to accept. If we lead reasonably moral and honest lives, we somehow feel it is God's duty to accept us. After all, we are bringing him a rather worthwhile gift in ourselves. The derelict's heart can avoid this problem: he can begin to understand his own worthlessness and come in a straighter line as a rule. God's pursuit may well be easier with the publican than with the Pharisee, simply because it is simpler for the publican to see that he cannot be other than he is until he knows God. The publican knows he is not doing God a favor; therefore it is simpler for him to recognize the favor of God. The confessed sinner glimpses the love of God—even for him—murmurs, "Thank you," and hears God answer, "You're welcome!"

God *can* welcome us into his presence just as we are because he knows that his redemption comes with the welcome: his redemption, his pardon, his cleansing, his forgiveness. And so it isn't what we bring, it is what God makes of what we bring that matters. "I know the thoughts I think toward you," saith the Lord. "They are thoughts of peace and not of evil; to give you an expected end." God knows what he is doing when he calls us and he knows what he can do in us after we respond to his call. He knows what he has in mind for each one who answers; he knows the "expected end." And, if we permit, he will go on "working his good pleasure" in us. But he does require our permission. "Behold, I stand at the door and knock." God never just opens the door and walks in. His welcome is universal—there are no exceptions, but we must also welcome him.

When we do welcome God, he comes quickly, bringing all we need in his own person. He does not enter our lives bearing a package of this or that. He does not bring *pardon* from our sins in one hand and *cleansing* from our sins in the other. He does not merely bring a bundle of *relief*. He brings himself and in him there is pardon, cleansing, relief. He is our pardon, he is our cleansing, he is our relief.

Compartmentalizing God is the weakening sin of Christendom. Like the Pharisees, who split the Law into a thousand pieces—even added to it from their own learned intellects—we Christians have done the same with the simplicity of the Gospel of Jesus Christ. He said, "I come that you might have life and have it more abundantly." He did not say, "I come bringing this and that to be portioned out to you as you grow in grace." Jesus came to simplify life, not to complicate it.

When he pardons us, he does not hand us *a pardon;* he enters our lives with his love and frees us. The Bible does not say, "If you accept this or that doctrine, you will be handed a helping of freedom." Jesus said, "If the Son shall make you free, you shall be free, indeed!" It is not the noun "pardon" that matters in the life lived with God, it is the action verb "to pardon"—an action of God himself contained in himself. His very presence pardons me. *He* is my pardoner. I must rely on *him* and not on a *pardon,* because I will need further pardoning as I live the years of my life on earth. I cannot be "free, indeed" unless the one who frees is continually with me, continuing to free me. You cannot be "free, indeed," unless the one who frees is continually with you, continuing to free you.

We cannot be clean unless Jesus, the cleanser, is with us to keep us clean. He does not hand us a "clean bill of spiritual health." He goes on keeping us clean. As clean as we want to be kept. "If we confess our sins, he is faithful and just to forgive us our sins, and to cleanse us from all unrighteousness." Our part is two-fold: We must see that true cleansing is available to us only in the person of Christ and we must recognize and confess our continuing need of his cleansing. This in itself frees us. We are not bound to observances in order to be cleansed. We are bound only to the freeing presence of the Son of God. It is he who is "faithful and just to forgive us our sins, and to cleanse us from all unrighteousness."

His pardon and his cleansing are all of a piece, all part of his person, all motivated by his love. They are also integral to his receiving us. He does not receive us and then decide whether or not he will pardon us, will cleanse and forgive us. *Everything we need is in the mind and the intention and the heart of God all the time.* He never receives without full intent to give.

And yet, we do not all possess the certainty of his pardon. We are not all cleansed at once. This is not God's fault. It is ours, either from lack of understanding or from lack of willingness, or that we do not yet know how to receive fully. We have forgotten how to be childlike. We tie strings to what we give and we remain convinced that God does the same. We fear, for example, that if we receive his complete gift of pardon, the very guilt we lose may cost us some attention from our friends. A fearful young woman once said to me: "If I go all the way with God, you and I won't have anything left to talk about. You'll stop seeing me. Stop writing to me." We don't receive fully from him because we prefer to keep one or two reins in our own hands, just in case. We close our hearts and our minds and our spirits before he is through giving because we are uneasy somewhere inside about what all that generosity might cost us in self-pity, in self-indulgence, in self concern. We don't want to learn how to come back swiftly from disappointment. We want to trust a little in our material security—not altogether, but a little: enough to keep us feeling successful. We choose to go on thinking life owes us a certain amount, and we like praise and promotion, so we turn away from him while he is still giving to us.

Our receptivity to God is also limited by our refusal to receive all those other people he loves just as much as he loves us. We are born *exclusive*. We find it easy to love and accept those who think the way we think, who have attained to our standards of living, who are our kind. There would have been no need for the Civil Rights Movement in America if every professing Christian had learned to receive fully from God. We cannot receive fully from him and refuse to receive our fellow human beings. There is no particular virtue in welcoming Negroes at the front door of our homes, of sharing our meals with them. No more virtue than in sharing with a Scottish or German friend. There *is* lack of Christianity in refusing to share with *anyone*.

Christians are supposed to be indwelt with the very Spirit of Christ himself. Can you imagine his refusing to welcome, to receive for any reason? We are not going to like and enjoy all members of every race on earth, because we are all different. But *if* our acquaintances happen to be Chinese, Italian, Japanese, Swedish, German, English, or Negro, they will all be welcome according to the depth of our relationship, *if* we have received fully from Christ. We function comfortably within the boundaries of our churches, our alumni associations, our lodges, our political and social groups. But if we set these limitations as class and racial distinctions, we are not receiving freely, as God receives us. We are being *exclusive* and God is always *inclusive*.

During the recent hectic and somewhat ridiculous Primary campaign waged in the state where I now live, a friend of mine, attempting to convince me to vote for a certain man, said, "Well, now, he isn't a segregationist as you think—he just isn't an integrationist." I laughed. There seemed nothing else to do.

Our God is the great integrator. His welcome is for everyone, and he commands us to love one another as he loved us. Jesus stayed in trouble with the segregationists—the "separatists"—when he was on earth. He ate with sinners and publicans. He had a long, enlightening talk with an outcast Samaritan woman, even going so far as to give her a chance to be gracious with him. He *asked* for a drink of water from her wellbucket, so he could put himself in the divinely humble position of receiving from *her*. Anyone who receives as fully as he knows how from God, can receive, and receive from anyone at any time under any circumstance.

The pardon of God cost far too much for us to refuse it. The heart of the God-Man torn open on the cross was far too costly for us to qualify the gift. Unless I am going to allow him to cleanse me fully, unless I mean to take up my cross too, and follow him, am I not showing flagrant ingratitude to take just what I want of his offering? To receive only what keeps me comfortable? If I am only going to love God because he saved me, does it really matter how many books I write praising that salvation? If I am willing to receive my concept of an eternal insurance plan and refuse to follow the Saviour anywhere, am I a Christian? It seems to me the rigidity, the snobbishness, the self-righteousness, the private-club atmosphere in some churches is largely caused by those who receive God's "salvation" but do not receive *him*.

Is this possible? I do not know. But I do know that the Christians who make me feel most welcome are those who speak often of the Saviour and almost never of *their* salvation, of their separation from the "world." No one knows better than I that "Christ Jesus came to earth to save sinners." No one needed a Saviour more than I needed him, but I was not drawn by his call to salvation, or to separation. I was drawn by his call to himself. It is wondrous that he receives us, that he pardons us, that he cleanses us. Still, to me, the eternal wonder is not that we are received, but that it is God who receives us. Shift the emphasis and see the difference:

Just as I am, thou wilt *receive.* . . .

Just as I am, *thou* wilt receive. . . .

It is "Wonderful, wonderful! That the one who has help to give is the one who says, Come hither!"

A welcome is a relieving thing. Much of the quiet suffering among us today is caused by not feeling welcome. Perhaps, if you live your life snugly within the sheltered margins of a safe home, within the safety of your selective social group, following one doctrinal line inside the set boundaries of your particular denomination, you do not realize how unwelcome many persons feel most of the time. But the unwelcome walk our streets and ride our transit systems and wait on us in stores and restaurants. If there were some way to create a universal human welcome, much of our heartache would end. Oh, but there is—the divine welcome is here, is everywhere, has always been. And it is set apart from any human welcome because it gladly invites us to come *just as we are.* This in itself is relief enough, but God never stops with just enough. He goes on.

His welcome is universal, his pardon complete, his cleansing thorough, but the *more* is the deepest *relief* of all: It is *God* who calls.

A man walks out of a courtroom after a human judge has pardoned him, relieved and exhilarated.

He is free from having to pay any penalty. Perhaps he had a clever attorney who got him off even though he was guilty, perhaps he had endured a false conviction. At the moment he leaves the courtroom a free man, this is almost beside the point. His relief is so great because he is free to walk out. Here the analogy breaks down. God has put all judgment into the hands of Jesus Christ. The human judge merely pronounces the pardon. He dismisses the case and the defendant. The judge makes no further effort in the man's behalf. But when God pardons, he doesn't stop there. He cleanses and keeps clean. He forgives and loves us forever. He goes with us, promising never to leave us, never to forsake us. "Lo, I am with you always. . . ." We can now use his strength, his sensitivity, his balance, his wisdom, his compassion. If we agree, we can even "let the mind that was in Christ Jesus" be in us. We can think from his viewpoint, with his attitude of heart. We are freed from the necessity of trying to do the impossible: to make sense out of life as we earthlings see it. There is no sense to anything until we begin to look from the viewpoint of God from the cross. There is no logic and no answer until we begin to think of all of life from the fact of redemption.

The great relief that fills the heart of the person who is willing to respond to the call of God is more, much more than the relief of pardon. It is the relief of the cleansed, strengthened daily life, but there is still more. The ultimate relief lies in the fact of God himself. Pardon is to be desired, cleansing is to be desired, but rest comes and total relief only when one begins to learn of the nature of the God who grants it.

Too many of us could never believe we are called merely to be *good*. Some of us would be bored with the whole idea. Others among us would show no interest whatever in being called by God to be *religious, pious*. Even the call to eternal life is more than the deeply troubled in this life care to contemplate. God knows all this and the great relief comes here: He calls us only to himself. Goodness, spirituality, eternal life, a new capacity for joy—all come to us as a result of our union with Christ.

Our part is to come and to stay with the One who himself can give us all we need. *We are not the determining factor;* God is.

This is the great relief.

11

Because Thy promise I believe, . . .

A promise is a covenant, a pledge from one person to another to do or not to do something specific.

Through all the years since man has known of God, he has clung to the promises of God, has memorized them so they would be at hand in times of emergency, of fright, of failure.

"The Lord is my rock, and my fortress, and my deliverer; my God, my strength, in whom I will trust; my buckler, and the horn of my salvation, and my high tower. I will call upon the Lord, who is worthy to be praised: so shall I be saved from mine enemies."

"In my distress I called upon the Lord, and cried unto my God: he heard my voice out of his temple, and my cry came before him, even into his ears."

"He healeth the broken in heart, and bindeth up their wounds. He telleth the number of the stars; he calleth them all by their names. Great is our Lord, and of great power: his understanding is infinite."

The list of the promises of God is almost endless. It is right that we cling to them, keeping ourselves open to his voice to us through them in the midst of our personal trials. It would be impossible to have too many of the promises of God "hidden in our hearts." They have been set down for us to use in our need. And indeed, the mere psychological effect of the sound of their words quiets us. There is strength—contagious strength—even in the literature of these promises. Many people lull themselves to sleep at night quoting the Twenty-third Psalm.

But psychology and beautiful literature both have limitations. Even the knowledge that these promises come from the Holy Bible is not enough to give them the content I believe God intends them to have for us. Not enough to give them the power we need in times of deep tragedy, of paralyzing fear, of suffering of any kind. I am aware that there are Christians who seem to be able to be satisfied with the "Authority of the Scriptures" in themselves. At least this is the way they communicate their faith to me. The Scriptures have "authority" only because of their Author. I knew the Twenty-third Psalm and John 3:16 and John 1:1 before I knew Jesus Christ. They had no effect on me whatever except to arouse my admiration for their literary value.

Now that I know something of the nature of the God behind them, they have continuously opening meaning for me.

Before I became a Christian I did not attend any church, but on occasion I did attend a funeral and I had heard and read the words of Jesus concerning life and death: "I am the resurrection, and the life: he that believeth in me, though he were dead, yet shall he live: And whosoever liveth and believeth in me shall never die." They were the appropriate, but (to me) meaningless words read or spoken at most Christian funerals. "Let not your heart be troubled . . ." angered me. It seemed a cruel statement to make in the presence of those who sat before the dead bodies of their loved ones, struggling to muffle their sobs through the strange, depressing mouthing of "just words."

At Christmas I enjoyed the beauty of the Scriptures which told what, to me then, was a lovely legend concerning the ancient birth of Christ. I sang lines from these Scriptures, these promises of a Saviour, and experienced the warm, happy lift everyone receives from the familiar sound of Christmas carols. At least I thought it was the same happy lift everyone received. But when I sang "God and sinners reconciled" on the first Christmas after I had met Jesus Christ as my own Saviour, I thought my heart would burst with joy!

Meaning had entered *with him* into the old, familiar phrases.

Promises make us feel encouraged or comforted or less fearful, but they have eternal meaning for us *only* if we know the Promiser. The merry Quaker saint Hannah Whitall Smith contended that things are not true merely because they are in the Bible. They are in the Bible because they are true. Promises are not valid merely because they are part of Holy Writ. They are valid because the character of the Almighty God backs them up. They are valid because *he* is the Promiser.

At my beloved father's funeral service, my broken heart began to sing at the old, once meaningless promise of Jesus: because my father believed in Christ, he was not dead. Even though his dear, wasted body lay there in that casket before me, I *knew* with no effort on my part that he would never die. "Though he were dead, yet shall he live." I knew this, not because I had somehow managed to create an enormous faith; I knew it because I had come to know Jesus himself. I had never remembered my father lying inert and dead. Every mental picture of him I have had since he went away has been one of life, of joy, of his dear eternal self active in the very presence of God. This is not true because I have become so spiritually advanced. It is true because every day I learn more about the God who promises and gives everlasting life.

My dread of death for myself as well as my loved ones before I knew Christ was almost pathological. That dread has almost vanished now. The pain of loss is not lessened, but when one no longer fears mere extinction when the body dies, the sting is indeed gone. Because Jesus Christ lives, my loved ones who are no longer here with me live too. There is no sudden chopping off of life. There is, because of Jesus Christ, the Great Going On.

John 3:16, which children learn in Sunday School, is now the foundation of my faith; "For God so loved the world, that he gave his only begotten Son, that whosoever believeth in *him* should not perish, but have everlasting life."

His promise I believe because of *him*.

The promise of eternal life is not merely something all good people, all proper people, all well-meaning people are supposed to believe. It is a fact; backed up by the very existence of God. Mention the Great Going On to someone who has just lost a loved one in death, and the change of expression on the grief-stricken face will be swift: either peace will return at once or a desperate look of "I hope you're right." There is no more certain way to dis-

131

cover how real God is to another human heart than to speak of the continuing life when physical death has recently struck.

Throughout the Bible we are told that God loves us, that he is a merciful God. That "his mercy endureth forever." That he is always listening for our cries, always ready to heal our broken hearts, to bind up our wounds. We are assured that "his understanding is infinite." That "he remembereth that we are dust." Again and again, as thoroughly as words can do it, we are offered the assurance of the comfort and the love and the mercy of God. ". . . even to your old age I am he: and even to hoar hairs will I carry you: I have made, and I will bear: even I will carry, and will deliver you." A promise I am already sealing in my own heart for future comfort. But how can we—especially how can a weakened, feeble, elderly person—find strength from this assurance of God's love and care unless the true nature of the Father is already known?

We are able of our own volition and intelligence to derive a sense of comfort from a beautifully worded phrase, but if we know God in Jesus Christ, we are *enabled by his spirit* to draw *life* from every word he speaks to us.

Unless we know personally the one who ". . . was wounded for our transgressions . . . was bruised for our iniquities . . ." how can we know that ". . . with his stripes we are healed"? It is, after all, not even the beautiful, sacrificial spirit in which Christ permitted himself to be bruised and chastised that gives meaning to his suffering for us. It is the identity of the one who hung there that matters: The man on his cross was God himself proving his love for us—just as we are. God himself giving substance and eternal verity to every word he speaks to us. When the heart inside an ill, aching, aged body lays hold of the fact of this kind of love *personally*, then he can believe that this God will carry him . . . will deliver him safely at the end of his earthly journey.

When the weary, burdened, rebellious, or fear-ridden mind realizes who it is who urges: "Come unto me, all ye that labour and are heavy laden, and I will give you rest . . ." response is natural. And within this all-inclusive invitation of Jesus lies the secret of being able to take his rest: ". . . learn of me. . . ." He knows us so well, he deliberately told us *how* to bring our weariness and burdens to him. He did not expect the weary mind to be able to concentrate on spiritual exercises at the moment of deep need: *he gave the key*, along with the invitation. It is as though he said: "Now, I know how tired you are, how many things are pressing upon you, how hard you've worked. I know you are too weary to quote Scripture or think through anything. I want you to come to me and let me help you, but I also know you can't even do that unless you know you can trust me. So, my child, my weary,

133

confused child—*learn of me*. Let me be myself with you right now and remind you of my love. Learn of me. Learn of me. And when you do, you will come to me of your own accord."

Paul wrote to his friends at the Ephesian church: "For this cause I bow my knees unto the Father of our Lord Jesus Christ, of whom the whole family in heaven and earth is named, that he would grant you, according to the riches of his glory, to be strengthened with might by his Spirit in the inner man; that Christ may dwell in your hearts by faith; that ye, being rooted and grounded in love, may be able to comprehend with all saints what is the breadth, and length, and depth, and height; And to know the love of Christ, which passeth knowledge, that ye might be filled with all the fullness of God."

Paul's own heart overflowed with love for his friends as he wrote his letter, urging the Ephesians to believe in the love of Christ. He loved them so deeply, he would not have tossed off a superficially expressed spiritual fillip to them. He did not simply say, "You must believe God loves you." He told them they must open themselves to the indwelling spirit of Christ himself: ". . . that Christ may dwell in your hearts by faith. . . ." In other words, that they should live as near him as possible, in order to "be able to comprehend," to *know* of his nature which is *love*. Paul, as Saul, had been drawn to this love when first he saw the risen Christ on the Damascus road. He had been hearing about God and serving God with all his might and intellect. Job said, "I have heard thee by the hearing of the ear, but now mine eye seeth thee." The Lord God used different means, but he got the attention of both Job and Saul. They had heard, but then they *saw* him as he is in the Redeemer.

Saul, as God's man, Paul, came to know his Redeemer so intimately, so well, that he stopped merely serving him and began to *live* him. "To me to live is Christ." So clearly did Paul come to see into the heart that broke on Calvary that he could write to the Christians in Rome: "For I am persuaded, that neither death, nor life, nor angels, nor principalities, nor powers, nor things present, nor things to come, nor height, nor depth, nor any other creature, shall be able to separate us from the love of God, which is in Christ Jesus our Lord."

Paul could know this to be true, he could know that the Lord God of Abraham and Isaac and Jacob, his ancestors, was a God whose mercy endured forever, who would carry him to his old age, who would daily deliver him. Paul could know that the Lord was his shepherd, and that he would be welcome in the house of the Lord forever, because he had come to know the Lord himself in Jesus Christ. He could know what Isaiah meant when he wrote: "Thou wilt keep him in perfect peace, whose mind is stayed on thee. . . ." Paul knew the Old Testament promises of peace could be relied upon because he had come to know the One who made them. Had come to know Christ well enough to know that "he is our peace." That he does not just give peace—he *is* our peace.

A promise of God to those who weep, who are hurt in body or in spirit—one of the most poetic passages in the Old Testament—is tucked within a rather long verse of II Kings: ". . . I have heard thy prayer, I have seen thy tears: behold, I will heal thee. . . ." Even its rhythm, its music, the lay of one word against the other has a quieting effect upon the grieving human heart. But there come to all of us those times when more than quiet is needed, when more than temporary solace is a necessity. To have anyone say to us: "I have heard you weeping and I want to do something to help," is a comfort. But when God bothers to say to us that *he* has seen our tears, more than mere comfort is at hand: healing begins because of his very nature. Often, because of our broken hearts, we tend to forget his power and to dwell on only his tenderness. But when the sound of our weeping is heard, power is vital—God's power, which can be administered to us in the quiet as well as in the storm. We are warped in our concept of power by our conditioning to the scientific knowledge of it for military and industrial use. It is easy to conceive of power in an atomic explosion, in the roar of mighty engines. But God's power opens the crocus as surely as it energizes the sun. The most startling show of power ever unleashed in all human history took place in the almighty meekness loosed by Jesus on his cross. God has no problem fitting his power to our need. "A bruised reed shall he not break, and smoking flax shall he not quench. . . ." When it is God who sees our weeping, we can believe his promise to heal us.

> Just as I am, Thou wilt receive,
> Wilt welcome, pardon, cleanse, relieve;
> Because Thy promise I believe,
> O Lamb of God, I come, I come!

We can come, certain of the great, glad welcome, the joyful pardon, the cleansing, the relief of no longer having to "go it" alone, *if we believe him to be a God of his word*.

And we can know him to be a God of his word if we will take the time to learn of him in Jesus Christ. "No man hath seen God at any time: the only begotten Son, which is in the bosom of the Father, *he hath declared him.*"

12

Just as I am, Thy love unknown . . .

The love of God is both unknown and known. It is both unknowable and knowable. We should not be surprised by the look of incredulity on the faces of those whom we try to convince of this love. They are right when they contend that there could be no way for mere man to discover the height and the depth of the love of God. There is no way. The *extent* of God's love is, to the earthling, unknowable. If it were possible to know, we could not endure the knowing. At times a few seem to get flashes of insight into the far reaches of his love, but the flashes pass as quickly as they come. We could not contain full knowledge of the love of God.

We are staggered at statistics concerning the immensity of the physical universe alone. Light years and galaxies flung beyond galaxies—even what will soon be the short flight of man in space on his way to the moon challenges our credulity. And yet all these physical phenomena of distance are a poor analogy in attempting to describe the love of God. It is not only poor, it is wrong. Love cannot be described by distance or by time or by calculations. It is eternal in its nature or it is not love. Surely, it is eternal or it is not the love of the eternal God.

Time confuses us here. We are caught in it and even though our intellects remind us that God is not caught in time—that with him there is no beginning and no middle and no end—our emotions trap us and unless in our peaceful moments we have learned to free God of time, the crisis moments find us in turmoil.

C. S. Lewis wrote in his *Letters to Malcolm:* "I certainly believe that to be God, is to enjoy an infinite present, where nothing has yet passed away and nothing is still to come." Viewed from our vantage point, this can give us insight on the sanity and the balance of God: he does not go to pieces in crisis times because he *is* in "an infinite present where nothing has yet passed away and nothing is still to come." To the unthinking among us, this would appear to be a state of nothingness. It is not. It is to know life that is capable of encompassing everything. As C. S. Lewis also suggests, those who have learned to do more than one thing at once can somewhat understand what this means. But most of us are one-tracked, capable of experiencing fully only one event at a time, one emotion, one idea, one concept.

To put God in the confines of our time belittles him. To keep ourselves trapped in time when he offers eternity *now* belittles him. Those who are capable of holding only one idea at a time to the exclusion of even the possibility that there might be a more truthful one somewhere around are refusing eternity. The bigots, both political and religious, are refusing eternity. The stubborn refuse it, and the hard-headed, who won't be taught, refuse it. This, of course, is why the unteachable (the unhumble) cannot know love, cannot receive it or give it. They are caught in the limits of their own notions, and love is never penned in, never static, never without motion.

When we confine God, we confine ourselves. We hold ourselves off from his love. We cannot hold God's love captive, but we can hold ourselves from it by attempting to decide once and for all that we already know the extent of his love. Anyone who holds to the idea that there is a limit to the love of God does not know him in Jesus Christ. Anyone who fears reprisal from God for walking in darkness has not looked deeply into the heart that was torn open on Calvary. The Christian's God does not deal in reprisals; he deals only in love. Not the soft, indulgent love that sentimentalizes and pampers, but the strong, tough love that held Jesus to his cross. The holy love that kept him sinless as he lived among us in this sinful world. Not the love that gives license, but the love that sets free. Not the love that gives itself because and only because we think we are pleasing God, but the love that gives because its very nature is love.

No man can know that the *extent* of the love of God, but any man can know its *nature*. That is why God's love is both unknowable and knowable. Our hope is in the *extent*—the height, the depth, the breadth of it—but our sure knowledge can rest in its *nature*. The nature God took every care to make plain to us in Jesus Christ. The love from which we *cannot* be separated. The love which covers our unanswered questions and makes the rough places straight. The love that loves us no matter what we're like.

Has it ever occurred to you how utterly and finally God trusts his own love? If he did not trust the transforming power of his love for us, how would he dare have given us free wills? How would he dare have given them in the first place, and more so, how would he dare permit us to retain them even after we have come to him? God and God alone knows the thoughts that he has toward us. God and God alone knows they are thoughts of good and not of evil and that they are designed to give us the end *God* expects for us. If we view all this from the perspective of our limited concepts of love, we see him as the eternal gambler. If I know myself at all, I know that "in me [that is, in my flesh] dwelleth no good thing: for to will is present with me; but *how* to perform that which is good I find not. For the good that I would I do not: but the evil which I would not, that I do." Left on our own, even under the influence of the highest human love, this is the way we are. God is fully aware of our predicament, although we act at times as though he is not aware at all. But he is also fully aware of the infinite cleansing and purifying power of his own love toward us. He trusts that love completely and, because his self-knowledge is also complete, he trusts his love never to turn from us, always to remain in motion toward us. And this love is moving toward us every minute of our time-trapped lives *just as we are*. It does not increase its flow on the days when we have held no unkind thoughts, have experienced a particularly meaningful prayer time, have done an unusually selfless thing. When we have been obedient, have concentrated on the very nature of God himself, we simply find ourselves *experiencing* the love that has been coming toward us *all the time*. God does not send more love when we behave. He loves because he is God and God is love and he loves us just as we are. Because of him, not because of us.

When our relationships with God are close and smooth and confident, we *discover* more of the love that has always been there for us, but it is not given then in greater measure. He has always given his love fully and he will always give it, and when we grasp this truth, the transforming power of that love can begin to touch us. We are freed daily because daily we break loose from the entrapment of time and enter the captivity of love where the limits are set safely by nothing but the *nature* of God.

And here the great simplicity takes over. The once crippling process of doing this and that because our particular group does it, of not doing this or that because our conditioning prohibits it, is no more. We have only one guide—the love of God. Within us, by his Holy Spirit, he prompts and checks, but his guidance is always by means of love because his Holy Sprit is the very person of God dwelling in us. God in our flesh, ready to live his life through us, ready to influence our decisions, to direct our thinking, and ready, too, to redeem our mistakes. The fact that his spirit lives in us in no way keeps us from human error. God's spirit *directs* our wills, but it does not bend them.

This is our part and the reason so many of us miss our cues from this ever present guide within us is because we fail to *continue* to learn of him. Events happen too fast for us to rush to the Scriptures for a refresher course each time a decision must be made, an action taken. Unless we take Jesus' word for the necessity of *learning of him constantly,* we will miss our directions. No one escapes wrong moves, but the indwelling Holy Spirit is the spirit of the redeemer God, and he will show us how to make use of the errors in our judgment.

Jesus, on the night before his crucifixion, assured his disciples that the Comforter (the Holy Spirit) would come, and he added: "I, myself, will come to you." The Holy Spirit, the Father, and the Son have one and the same nature, so there is no reason whatever for us to doubt that the spirit of God within us is still a redeemer God who will in his own way and in his own time show us how to make redemptive use of our mistakes. His love has always been and will always be a redemptive love because God's nature does not change. Only those who have not learned this waste time fretting over mistakes.

The love of God and the love of Christ are one and the same love. They are not two similar loves; they are the same love. And this love is made available to us in the only way we can accept love—through another person: the person of the Holy Spirit. So, when we speak of the love of God in its fullest, most accurate sense, we speak of love as demonstrated in Jesus Christ. And the love of Christ *is* knowable. We cannot fathom its extent, but we can learn its nature so that we can begin to know something of the expected end God plans for us. Just as we learn to live with another human being by taking the time to learn his character traits, so we learn to live with Christ. Because his very own spirit lives in us, and because he came to our earth to live among us, we *can* learn. We can know the *nature* of his love and then and only then will we trust its *extent*. Then and only then can we begin to experience eternal life *now*. God does not think our world has collapsed when we lose a loved one in death, or when our hearts are broken for any of a number of reasons. He *knows* it seems that way to us and he is the only healer of broken hearts, but he lives "in the infinite present" and works on our behalf accordingly. He knows what creative good he, the redeemer God, will bring out of our heartbreak *if* we trust his love for us. I do not see how those whose hearts are crushed by tragedy can go on living without a sure knowledge of the redeemer of God! They do, but is it really living? Isn't life then, after the tragedy, merely a desperate effort to substitute for what is lost?

Paul said: "For the love of Christ constraineth us. . . ." What did he mean? The dictionary says of this word "constrain": *to compel, force; to secure by bonds, to confine.* Is this a freeing thing? Yes, when one knows the nature of the love of Christ, there is no freedom outside its restraints, outside its compelling, its bonds. When trouble strikes, only the love of Christ can force us into the needed control of our emotions. More than the meaning of *force* as we have come to think of it, there is in the love of Christ the same quick energy as the force used in a sudden rescue. A friend once told me of the superhuman burst of strength that came to her when she found her mother overcome by gas in a room with no air in it. She *forced* open a window which had been stuck for years and saved her mother's life. The love of Christ within us forces us to go on breathing, forces the oxygen of new life, new reason for living into us. "I wanted to jump down into that new grave with my wife, but something kept me from it. Something inside me kept me needing to live out my own life. It was like a force I could not resist." This grief-shattered man knew Christ personally. This knowing did not diminish his agony at the death of his beloved wife, but he was aware of an inner force that compelled him to go on. The Weymouth Translation of the passage from Paul's Second Letter to the Corinthians declares that "the love of Christ overmasters us. . . ." It does. He is the Master and when we need to be overmastered, only he can do it. In the New English Bible we read Paul's words: "For the love of Christ leaves us no choice. . . " It is as though, when we are without strength, without human reason for living, we are given no choice but to permit the love of Christ to take over for us, in us.

The Phillips interpretation perhaps is all-inclusive: "The very spring of our actions is the love of Christ." Does this imply that our every action is, if we have entered into a personal relationship with him, going to be Christlike? Obviously not. We are still in the driver's seat where our wills are concerned. But God does *not* expect the impossible of us; he only expects us to expect the impossible from him. *If* we have learned something of the *nature* of Christ's love, we will know that in our own lives when going on seems impossible to us, the love of Christ will overmaster us, will *force* us from within to choose the way of life over the way of death. If "the very spring of our actions is the love of Christ," it is indeed as though we have no choice but to give his love freedom to act in our behalf. We err when we attempt the futile task of *trying to act Christian*. There is no such thing. This is humanly impossible. But since "with God all things are possible," the secret lies in our trusting his love enough to expect him to compel us in the creative way, never the destructive.

One thing we must know and refuse to relinquish is the irrevocable fact that *nothing* can separate us from the love of Christ. In no way does this mean that we will all go about always aware of his love, always feeling loved, protected, watched over. We won't. Up to a point we control our feelings, but only up to a point. Feelings have a way of taking us over when we are ill, weary, worried, disappointed, grieved. At those times we feel separated from the love of Christ. We pray and our words seem to go no higher than the ceiling. We hear nothing from him. We sense only our own lostness. We are not lost, if once we have placed our faith in the Good Shepherd. We feel lost, but we are not. His purusit of our hearts has not lessened. His love has not slackened, has not diminished. It is there as full and strong and persistent as ever. We do not feel it, but *it is* or God's Word is false, because it says *nothing* can separate us from the love of Christ. But the knowledge of the constancy of this love comes only after our *faith* has been actively placed in him. Faith and faith alone is our part, and faith *is trust in God himself,* a state of being which can come only from the continuing relationship. We cannot expect ourselves to possess robust faith if we turn to Christ only in times of conscious need. We will not be separated from his love, but we will have grown unaware of its constancy. We will have grown vague about his heart, his character. Robust, mature faith cannot be whipped up in a flash. It is the simply inevitable result of continuing friendship with Christ. *The more intimately we know him, the more certainly we trust him.*

Even if you know nothing of his love now, you can still come—just as you are. At this first turning, he takes the initiative for us. It is he who seeks us out, draws us to himself with love. Anyone who turns to him will find him, and then faith and continuing knowledge of his love begin—the love from which nothing can ever separate us. The love that cannot pass away because it "enjoys an infinite present." The love whose *extent* is unknown, but whose *nature* is altogether knowable in Jesus Christ, the Lamb of God.

13

. . . Thy love unknown
Hath broken every barrier down; . . .

A barrier is simply anything that hinders approach;
anything that fences in, keeps back. With our world
grown so "small" we are more and more aware of
the language barrier. Thousands of words are written about the communications barrier between individuals, due mainly, I suppose, to the very super-
ficiality of our living—our inclination to speed, to
quantity, to conformity. "Religion" is popular, but
it is as though our privacy has been invaded, or at
least some rule of good manners broken if God or
sin or the afterlife enters polite conversation. We

are twentieth-century surface-skimmers, finding our meager comfort in staying near the top of everything—it's "safer" that way even within the marriage bonds.

Two of my best friends turn into different people from the ones I know when they are in the company of their wives. Neither man is unhappily married. There just seems to be a communication barrier between each husband and each wife. I have been stimulated by long conversations with both men in the company of one or two other persons, but a kind of distance appears when their charming wives are with us. Obviously there is intellectual imbalance with both couples, but there is more too. There is surface-skimming amounting almost to shyness.

What can the love of God do about breaking down a barrier like this? Nothing, most likely, until these two husbands and wives begin to share God with each other. Heaven knows politeness is better than argument, but if courtesy and fidelity and the children are the only bonds, only a fragment of love is operating. I grieve for these four people because they are missing so much together.

Thy love . . . hath broken every barrier down. How?

How does the love of God break down barriers? How does the love of God knock down fences that keep us from each other on the deeper levels of our beings?

How does the love of God break apart the thick walls of political and religious disagreement which shut one group of human beings off from another?

How does the love of God dissolve the obstacle that prevents real oneness between a man and his wife? Between friends?

There is no answer to any of these questions until we come to see first of all something of how the love of God has removed every barrier between his heart and the human heart.

"I try to pray, but I can make no contact with God. It is as though there is a high barricade between us. I am on one side and he is on the other."

"I am aware of the fact of God. I am not fighting faith in him, but how do I get over the hurdle?"

When God came to earth in the person of his Son, Jesus Christ, he did not at that time *begin* to remove the barriers between himself and his human children. From our Father's side there were no barriers in the first place. When he came to earth in Jesus Christ, he came demonstrating the fact that the barriers were nonexistent!

In a letter last week, I read: "I think God is there—out there somewhere—but how can I ever be sure? I mean, how can I know I've managed to reach him? I want to make the effort, but I'm afraid I'll fail to bridge this awful gap between us."

If this state of mind were not so tragic, so destructive, so pathetic, I'd be tempted to answer: "Nonsense." Because when one takes time to look at Jesus Christ, all of these arguments against the potential of making contact with the living God fall away. If some gigantic, superhuman effort on our part were needed in order to reach God, would his personal revelation of himself, Jesus Christ, have called himself the Good Shepherd? Does a good shepherd expect his lost sheep to seek out the shepherd? Does he sit down comfortably by the fire and watch while the hungry, frightened, endangered lamb struggles through the brambles and over the high rocks that separate them? Does he wait, tapping his staff on the ground impatiently while the helpless lamb scrambles in circles trying desperately to find his way back to the fold?

Does God, the Good Shepherd, sit benignly on some distant, gold-encrusted throne and tap his celestial foot while we fight and work and suffer and climb in our helpless efforts to reach what to us all is our ultimate home? Did the prodigal's father sit inside his splendid house with the solid doors locked and peer through heavy lace curtains at his stumbling son coming home? The boy was still "a great way off"—not even in sight of his father's house—when he saw his father *running* to meet him. The prodigal had his speech of repentance all made up. He knew what he would say, hoping desperately that he would be permitted to stay on as a mere servant in the house where he had grown up. He didn't dare hope his father would welcome him back as a son. He barely hoped to be accepted as a menial.

And this is a clue to those of us who insist upon struggling home to the Father. Who insist that there is a barrier to climb over. We are aware of our guilt, our unworthiness, but seemingly unaware of the Father's heart. Seemingly unaware that he in no way expects us to shine ourselves up, to improve our dispositions, to untangle our selfish motives. The reason he does *not* expect any of this from us seems to escape us entirely. Remember, God does not expect self-improvement from us first; God welcomes us *just as we are* because he knows our helplessness. We can assume responsibility for ourselves, in fact we can insist upon it to the extinction of other people in our lives, and feel quite adequate to life. We can pay our bills and vote in every election and serve our communities and write checks for charity and feel worthy. But when we look deeply into our own natures, we see so much against which we are utterly helpless, so much that is unlike God, we begin foolishly to fret and struggle, attempting to remedy some of this *first*.

Jesus said quite plainly: "You must be born again." Does this sound like a complicated course in self-improvement? Does this sound as though we must find a way to rid ourselves of our own fears, our own fightings, our own problems and then come to God?

Even after we come, we are still helpless and the sooner we realize that conscious helplessness in the human heart in the presence of the living God is the healthiest possible climate for spiritual growth, the sooner we begin to grow.

God does not even hint at the necessity for us to do anything but come as we are. He does not because there is no other way to come. If we come proud of our generosity, we are, in that area, not coming to God, but *playing God*. If we come proud of our morality, we are only erecting a barrier on our side, but there is never, never a barrier on the side of God. Somehow we must rid ourselves entirely, once and for all, of the last remnant of the false notion that there is a single person in all the world not good enough to be a Christian. Becoming a Christian has nothing whatever to do with being good. Becoming a christian has to do with God. And with him there are no barriers. No fences. No requirements but the recognition of our own need of a Saviour.

And yet, I believe we have put too much stress on our sinfulness and not enough on the love of God. To speak only of the love of God and never of our need of a Saviour is false. No religious philosophy erects barriers from our side so quickly as to give a man or a woman the impression that because God is love, nothing else is important. Sin is important and sin is one condition we all share. "All have sinned and come short of the glory of God." But

Jesus died for us all, too, and it is reasonable to believe that more people would find a way out of their guilt if they were shown something of the true nature of this Man-God who hung on his cross for our freedom. We must be aware of our need for forgiveness, but at the same instant, we must look at the heart of God. One without the other creates a barrier. The finger pointed in condemnation at sin can sink a man, can twist him dangerously from the whole person God intended him to be in the first place. Wide, sweeping declarations of the love of God erect barriers just as surely, because there is no access to awareness of this love, no access to the freedom it offers *until,* conscious of our sin and our guilt, we come to him for pardon.

"The middle wall of partition" between God and man has never existed except on the side of man. And once any human heart is exposed to the love of God as it is given to us in Jesus Christ, all barriers go down. There is a fire about God's love that melts them down.

The human barrier of extreme self-concern perhaps keep more of us from God than any other, if we dare to be honest. And yet self-concern as such is difficult to change unless we are aware of some of its legitimate causes. The state of chronic self-concern is often misunderstood. There are cheerful, generous persons deeply sorry for themselves, but unaware of why. An intelligent look at a few under-

157

standable barriers which keep us from God puts an immediate end to our trite, generalized picture of the self-absorbed person. The self-absorbed person is *not* necessarily neurotic, whimpering, unattractive. His reasons for unconscious self-concern may be legitimate, but he will remain self-occupied until he becomes God-occupied.

Our individual identities are our most prized possessions, and *apprehension over the possible loss of one's identity* can lead directly to self-occupation—and become a barrier to keep us from God. It was for me. Somehow I feared that if I gave myself to Jesus Christ, I would of necessity grow to be like some of the other Christians I knew. This, of course, is false, but it causes us to balk just the same. At that point we do not understand that this is an imaginary barrier erected by our own tendency to classify ourselves, to become carbon copies of each other. The last thing God intends is for us to lose our identities. We are to lose our headstrong battle for identity, but once we lose it to him, inevitably we *gain our true natures*. God has created no two persons alike and he has no intention whatever of revising his creation. His desire is to redeem us— to bring us back to what he meant us to be in the first place. We are apprehensive about the loss of our own individuality if we lose our lives to Jesus Christ, but it *is* an absurd barrier—a needless one. And once again, we will find that it can be broken down for each one of us through knowledge of the nature of God. He does not want duplicate copies; he wants originals.

Young people in particular tend to pity themselves if they are forced into a religious mold by their elders. God understands this. No one can deny that we do live in an *amoral society*. Morality has gone out of style. I am at the moment working on research for a novel laid in the ante-bellum era of the American South. Constantly, I am puzzled as to how I can be authentic in writing of the rigid social mores of that period and still make it believable to middle-twentieth-century readers. It *is* a different world in which we live and the identity so valued by young people is challenged right and left by the thought of trying to live a Christian life in the swinging amoral society around them. Here again, we confront the necessity of learning first hand of the true nature of God in Jesus Christ. God does not impose rules upon us: He motivates us from within. If we simply do not enjoy something, do not want to do it, think it ludicrous, there is no problem in abstaining. A first-hand insight into what God is up to in our lives will show us that he is not interested in our becoming like all the other church people any more than he is interested in our conforming to the world. Left on our own, we simply do not have the strength to be different, but God does not leave us on our own. He is *in* every activity, every effort to succeed, every vicissitude *with* us—*not* forcing us into a pattern, not trying to "make us religious"—rather, he is about the exciting business of making us *real*.

Every minute of our lives lived in our so-called amoral society we must remember that God is not old-fashioned. Neither is he afraid of what is going to happen to us. We are in his hands and since he is not caught in time, God is always contemporary. He was contemporary in the Middle Ages and in the beginning and he is contemporary now. God's pursuit of the human heart cannot be measured by the morality in evidence around us—or by the lack of it. God is no more shocked at our amorality than he was at the superficial morality of the Victorian era. He wants us to be our best selves, unlike anyone else, fully creative—not lost in the shuffle of social proprieties or improprieties.

Another barrier which God has already broken down is the barrier of our *fear of the unknown*. All these barriers are strangely related. Nothing can cause us to feel more concerned for ourselves than fearing what we do not know. We tend, quite understandably, to fear what might happen to us when we are old, to fear our money will run out, to fear our jobs will end, to fear illness—to fear for the actual survival of the human race. Every thinking person now and then shares the inner fear (often not spoken) that man will, in the madness of the arms race, wipe the human race from the earth.

Would God permit this to happen?

I don't know. No one knows but God and, in the

realm of our fears of the unknown especially, there is no other alternative but to learn and learn and learn of the nature of the God who holds the universe in his hands. I do not know any more than you know what will happen to you, to me—to our world. But intelligent faith warns us we had better begin to stop wasting energy trying to find out about future *things* and *events* and begin to find out about the One who began it all. The One who dared to call himself the beginning *and* the end. We need not fear the end of our world—whether we bring it about or whether God brings it about, simply because God *is* the end and to be frightened of him is insanity. He will be there whatever happens and if we *know him* as he is, that will be enough.

All this *has* to sound glib to you if you are not centered down in the person of God himself. As glib as to say that he has also broken down another barrier behind which millions of persons honestly hide from God: the understandable refusal to come to a God who permits *continuing wars*. "I cannot give my life to a God of peace and love, why does he permit this slaughter to go on century after century?" The young woman who said this had just lost her husband in a short skirmish in a rice paddy in Vietnam. The "casualties were light." But her life had been torn apart.

Why, indeed, does God go on permitting wars century after century? Why does he go on permitting sin?

There are profound theological answers to these questions, I'm sure. It is enough for me to believe that God is in the process still—just as certainly as he was while his Son hung on the cross—of bringing us back to himself. By permitting wars where thousands of young men are killed? Where even women and children and elderly people are burned and murdered by falling bombs? No. He is about the business of continuing redemption by permitting man to go on living—man makes war, not God. *But* simultaneously he is also continuing his relentless pursuit of every human heart. God could not put an end to war without putting an end to man. God's peace is an inner peace, brought about by each of us responding for himself to God's call. He does not "save" nations en masse. He saves people— person by person.

If, to you, God is a superior force for good somewhere in infinity, then I can understand your thinking he should simply turn off the war-switch. But God is not merely a superior force for good. He is God—the living Redeemer, who is doing all he possibly can to bring peace the only way it can be brought—by redemption of individual human lives.

It is, of course, impossible for us to "get the big picture" God has of human destiny. But the more we find out about his nature as we learn of Jesus Christ, the more we become convinced that God does see the "big picture," that he has a plan—not a new one, but a continuing one for the salvation of his sinful children.

This redemptive plan of God's is in operation in the area of *social injustice* too, still another barrier to coming to the Father. It may not seem that way to those who spend themselves trying to help the underprivileged peoples of our world, but the plan is there—set in motion by God himself from the beginning. We forget that God is omniscient, that he has known from the beginning how things were going to be in the twentieth century. We plead for him to intervene when he has been in the midst of it from the moment he said to his Son, Jesus: "Let us make man in our image."

With all my heart, I am behind the authentic anti-poverty and literacy programs everywhere in the world; I believe God is, too. But in the long run, love will win the battle over human suffering as one after another of earth's children turn *personally* to the Father. We "are complete in him"—but only in him.

If your apprehension over the possible loss of your identity, your confusion about how to live in our amoral society, your fear of the unknown, your rebellion against continuing wars and social injustice are barriers which keep you from answering the call of the Lamb of God—they have already been broken down by the very God who calls you. They may seem to stand there for you, tall, solid,

163

impenetrable. They will still seem to stand there *until* you know enough about the God who calls to make the leap of faith. Once you take it, you will find them disappearing. This does not imply that anyone should wait until he has learned enough about God's nature to come. It is enough for the initial leap of faith to know that the Lord God has come to us in the person of Jesus Christ. But after the first response to his call, we must all begin and continue the one essential effort: to learn all we possibly can learn about what this God is really like.

We are not called by a God of vengeance, or a God with a rule-book in his hand. The God who calls us knew that the only real response to his call would come in a personal response to *his person.* "I, if I be lifted up . . . will draw all men unto *me."* He was lifted up in his Son, Jesus Christ, who hung on a cross because of our evil and his love. Hung there declaring to us in effect that evil cannot outlast love; that death cannot kill life.

The love poured out on Calvary *has* broken every barrier down. Our part is to believe it—to come to him and find out for ourselves that the door has been opened to the Father's house all along because nothing can close it. Jesus Christ *is* the door and he is alive forever and he will never change.

14

Now to be Thine, yea, Thine alone, . . .

What does it mean to give oneself wholly to God? What does it truly mean to be his and his alone? We can only know a thing to the limits of our ability to know, but since God only expects us to act on what we do know, our part is to be honest. Honest with ourselves, which means we are being honest with God.

We seldom reach the place of considering Christianity in a personal way unless, we cling desperately to all our rights to ourselves, but at the same time we are bored and distraught with our own management. One thing or another has happened to bring us to the place of recognizing our need of a Saviour. We may have made a fiasco of our emotional lives, our domestic lives, our financial affairs. We are afraid, somehow uneasy at the thought of going on year after year in the old way. Our best-made resolutions last a month or two at the most, and then we find we lack the power to change ourselves. We admit this before God if we are honest. We know we will go on gossiping and overeating and worrying and competing in spite of the fact that the cost will be greater than we are willing to pay. We know we will keep driving ahead toward that selfish goal, regardless of our guilt at causing other people to suffer for our overriding ambition. We dislike, even hate, ourselves for being as we are, but the unhealthy self-love is in command. The ancient story repeats its wearisome plot in us daily, *until* we reach the place of willingness before God.

I have recently witnessed a genuine conversion to Jesus Christ in the life of one of my dearest friends. In her middle years, after a materially successful life during which she attended church rather regularly, was well liked by most people, seemed outwardly to have no problems, she grew sick of her inner self. When I asked her yesterday what she did when she finally became God's and God's alone, she replied quickly: "I repented! You *have* to repent. I tried everything else and nothing worked. You *have* to repent."

We do. And the need for repentance goes on. It is not enough to repent initially. Repentance is not a thing we do for God's sake. It is a thing God waits for us to do for our own sakes! True repentance means that we have reached the place where we earnestly want God to take over for us. He does not wait for certain words from us, but he does wait, of necessity, for us to see that there is only one way to live fully, abundantly—and that way is to forsake ourselves for him. To forsake oneself does not mean to lose interest in life. It means just the opposite: When we have lost our lives in God's life, we are free at last to *be* interested in living as never before.

The new birth requires initial repentance, but there is no guarantee that we will not stumble again and again into old, self-indulgent ways. I do and so do you, even after years and years of living with Jesus Christ. The need for repentance goes on—not to please a touchy God, but because true repentance means we have seen more deeply into our steady need of him.

Often we hear the question: *"How* do I give myself to God?" I have come to believe that this is a dodge, not an honest question. My friend who has so recently given herself to him agrees. She asked, "How?" over and over again until she was really ready and then, quite alone with Christ, she knew perfectly well what was required for her to give herself wholly to him. She needed no other human being to prod her, to explain. Like me, she is not

167

JUST AS I AM

theologically trained and no amount of high-sounding rhetoric would have helped her. There was a meeting of two hearts—hers and Christ's—and repentance came to her mind immediately. We are, none of us, like another human being on earth; therefore to hold out a pat procedure or to insist upon certain phraseology is futile. Even if there are people around, at the moment the human heart meets the Saviour Jesus Christ, they are *along together*. And they both know.

Almost no one reaches this place of honesty before God without a battle. When we get down to basics in the areas of our own weaknesses, the fighting begins. And this is why we *must* begin with the bigness of God—the bigness of his love for us. True, his is a "love unknown" in its extent, but in Jesus we can know its characteristics. In Jesus we can know that God is not easily shocked. In Jesus we can know his willingness to go all the way with us, beginning just as we are.

Perhaps a rereading of Chapter 12 would be helpful. Because unless and until we have some grasp of the *fact* that there is no end, no running out of the love of God, we will not, indeed we cannot, give up our unhealthy self-love which we may be expressing in so-called self-hate.

A human being safe in the love of the Father will begin to learn how to love himself rightly, will begin to share God's genuine concern for his well-being. Will begin to want to live creatively, no longer bent on self-destruction for the love of a moment's pleasure, a moment's indulgence.

God, we must remember, "enjoys an infinite present." He is not caught in our today. With him there is no relief in putting things off until tomorrow; no joy in taking *now* what will surely bring pain later. The life surrendered to Christ learns how to live in the *eternal now*. We do not learn easily. The most righteous among us will grab one more momentary delight, planning to begin our growth in God "next week" as those of us who are overweight plan to begin to diet every Monday morning. As the excessive drinker rationalizes: "I'll *have* to get sober in time to get back to work, so why not make the most of the weekend?" The life given to God does not let tomorrow take care of itself: The life wholly God's is beginning, at least, to live in the *eternal now* with him.

Once we have seen that nothing is required for our reception by God but his call to us, once we have seen that there is no need to wait—no need to try to change ourselves, no need "to rid my soul of one dark blot . . ." no need to quiet our own fears and end our own doubting—once we have seen this, we can come to him. We can dare to be specific about our areas of self-absorption and the necessity for having them transformed.

There is no other place to start but at the point

of honesty. And this involves much more than merely returning too much change handed one by a weary restaurant cashier. It involves much more than paying one's honest debts. More than relinquishing the convenience of the small "white lie" to get out of something we don't want to do. It involves our very inner *integrity*.

To belong to Christ and Christ alone means, first of all, that we will begin to see all of life from *God's viewpoint* and no longer from our own. The building contractor who cuts corners in order to increase his profit does not belong to God and God alone. He belongs to himself. The manufacturer who tricks up his advertising so that his product is misrepresented to a gullible public is saving his own neck at the expense of other people whom God loves as much as he loves the manufacturer. The TV repair man or the garage mechanic who finds a way to pad his bill by replacing parts which don't need replacing is looking from his own viewpoint, not God's. And what of the performing musician or the writer who does not give time and energy and study enough to keep his work fresh? Who gets by the easy way on professional tricks in order to avoid the effort of steady improvement? What of the parents who give their children *things* instead of confidence and encouragement? What of the clergyman who rushes into his study on Saturday

170

afternoon and leafs frantically through another clergyman's published sermons to find a shortcut for Sunday morning?

To belong to God and God alone involves every area of our personal integrity and starts us looking at everyone and everything *from the viewpoint* of God first. And when we do this, we find to our surprise that a great simplification has taken place within us. To look first from the viewpoint of God automatically gives us a starting place. We "know which way to turn" when trouble comes, when problems pile up suddenly. Reckoning first of all on God in any situation clarifies, untangles. When legal complications or continuing failures or disappointments come, there is no wild rush from place to place hunting a way out. The first concern of the life given wholly to God is to stop long enough to discover the viewpoint of heaven on the entire matter. We are not to be fools, but neither are we to panic or to begin to fight back hammer and tongs. There is no need to do either *if* we have begun to look at all of life, *before the trouble comes,* from the viewpoint of God.

The life given wholly to God really *prefers harmony* to discord. If this sounds strange, think about it. Don't you know persons who seem to thrive on stirring up disharmony? A widower in his sixties once told me: "I was doing fine until my daughter

171

and her husband came to visit me last summer. She found everything wrong with the way I was living. I didn't keep house right, I worked too hard, the house was too big for me—I should sell it and move South and so on and on. By the time those children left, I had put my beloved home on the market and it was a month or two later before I quieted down enough for God to get me to seeing things his way again. This house is where I belong. This is where I was happy with my wife. I don't want to move and I don't need to, but I was in a terrible state of confusion for weeks after they left."

"Blessed are the peacemakers," Jesus said. Blessed are those who bring harmony with them, who long for harmony because peace cost God so much on the cross. The person whose life is centered in Jesus Christ will always hunt the peaceful way through every problem; will not compromise love for the sake of seeming peace, but will seek peace as the ultimate goal of every situation. The life given wholly to God will hunt always for the common bonds, never for the points of difference. It will be intent on building and never tearing down.

The man or woman who has become God's and God's alone, will always have a *refuge*. Christians are accused by non-Christians of being escapists. Some are. But the authentic follower of the Lamb of God, because he does have a refuge—a place to go *first,* not as a last resort—is far less troublesome to have around. He is not so likely to harass his friends and relatives with his troubles, not so likely to have his feelings hurt at the drop of a thoughtless remark, not so likely to be a trouble-maker—far less prone to anxiety. He is looking first from the viewpoint of God, and he already *has* a refuge, a place to which to take his problems, Someone with whom to think them through.

When tragedy strikes, the Christian whose life is no longer his own responsibility has an unshakable refuge in the Lord God. He has been found. He is no longer lost. He is at home already when the tragedy strikes. His grief is not heightened by having to hunt wildly for comfort. He already belongs to "the God of all comfort." When a Christian whose life has been given over to God is mistreated, wronged, he will be hurt, but he does not need to waste energy defending or pitying himself. *God* is "his shield and his buckler." He has known for a long time that "the battle is the Lord's" and not his.

The person who gives his life to God so that he belongs to Him and Him alone, does not stop with mumbling, "Thy will be done on earth as it is in heaven." He goes about *doing* the will of God to the limits of his understanding and as he does, he begins to understand more and more *why* this or that *is* the will of God. Anyone who has begun to comprehend the meaning of being His and His

173

alone, will begin to act quite naturally with the very intelligence of God—seeing His eternal purpose in the daily round.

A middle-aged woman wrote: "I think I'm in the will of God. But most of the time I just don't know." I don't believe this for one minute. If our minds are reasonably normal minds, we *know* when we are in the will of God *if* we are, so far as we know, wholly his. We confuse ourselves unnecessarily by worrying about irrelevant specifics where God's will is concerned. I don't think it matters to him whether the work we do is in the north or the south, the east or the west. What concerns God is the attitude of our hearts while we do that work. We sit around with pencil and pad and demand that God give us the address and the telephone number, when his concern is our inner integrity, our viewpoint, our love of harmony and peace, our assurance that he is our only safe refuge. When we have satisfied his concern in these areas, we are his and his alone. And we know his will.

Anyone who belongs to God *will love*, and this love will not stop with the family circle, the social or religious group in which we function most comfortably. If we do not want the inconvenience and the stretching required to learn to love with the all-inclusive love of God, there is little point in attempting to give ourselves to him. He demands nothing less. If our hearts and minds are closed when first we come, we may be sure he will attempt to open them both—wide. But it is wise to face the fact that when we give ourselves to the living God in Jesus Christ, we give *everything we are*.

Of course, in return we receive *everything he is*.

15

O Lamb of God, I come, I come.

"Behold the Lamb of God who taketh away the sins of the world."

Who is he? If he takes away the sins of the world, how is it that the world is seemingly destroying itself with sin two thousand years after the Lamb of God died on his cross?

How is it that nation is armed against nation, race against race? How is it that civilization has gone ahead by leaps and bounds in every area except the area of brotherhood and peace? How is it that if the Lamb of God came into the world to take away its sins, those sins are still rampant? If the young man on the cross at Calvary *was* God become man, if the heart torn open there *was* the manifestation of the very heart of the redeemer God, why is suffering not at an end? If he was the Prince of Peace, why, two thousand years after his coming, is war still in every headline and on every tongue? If there is no greater power in the whole of creation than the power of the almighty meekness of God, why is that power seemingly choked off from us? Why do men still wound and kill and cheat and conquer the helpless? Why is there still hunger and poverty and sickness and death? If the ground at the foot of the cross of Jesus Christ *was* level, why do some men still struggle for all the years of their earthly lives and never experience anything but want and misery? Is it that they are less in the sight of God than those who prosper and grow fat? Did God's great act of redemption at Calvary fall short of its purpose?

Wasn't its purpose to take away the sins of the world? To put an end to selfishness and greed and hypocrisy? Didn't Jesus, the Christ, say he came so that men would be free? Would know the abundant life? Was he wrong about his mission? Was he a fake? Was he just not quite adequate in what he did?

Here we can draw a definite line. Either he was or he was not God's revelation of himself. Either Jesus of Nazareth was God in human form or he

178

was not. Christians believe he was. He claimed to be and we take his word for it. We believe him to be "very God of very God," God incarnate come to live among man in order to make himself accessible even to the most humanly insignificant. If Jesus Christ was God become man, then he could not have been inadequate to his task. No one needs an inadequate God. Better to embrace humanism and lean on our own efforts, our own abilities, our own power than to attempt to follow an incompetent God. Better to grasp our human successes, to cling to our material gains and our intellectual achievements and let it go at that, if God can fail. No human being can convince another human being even of the existence of God, to say nothing of His power to succeed. God alone can do this, and so we waste our energies when we try. We can attempt to communicate what we have found to be experientially true, but we cannot prove God, nor can we prove his victory on Calvary. Man is prone to look at the evidence around him and if we look at the sins of the world in which we live, we see no proof that God took them away. They are still there in abundance. Instead of abundant life we see abundant sin and suffering and tragic inequality.

If you are looking at the world around you, even at the personal lives of the Christians you know, you will not find proof of God's success in the act of redemption. If you believe what is written in the Holy Bible, you will believe that God succeeded:

"For it pleased the Father that in him [in Jesus Christ] should all fulness dwell; and, having made peace through the blood of his cross, by him to reconcile all things unto himself; by him, I say, whether they be things in earth, or things in heaven. And you, that were sometime alienated and enemies in your mind by wicked works, yet now hath he reconciled in the body of his flesh through death. . . ." The Apostle Paul believed this to the extent that he lived and died by its truth.

But Paul lived long ago. What of *now?* What of us now? What has happened to the great reconciliation of God?

Nothing has happened to the great reconciliation of God. The power of Calvary has not diminished. The redemptive act of God in Jesus Christ can no more lessen than God can be lessened. As long as the redeemer God remains the redeemer God, *redemption holds.* It is we who have refused to "Behold the Lamb of God who taketh away the sins of the world." Even those of us who have entered into a personal relationship with him use him to our own ends, thus reversing the flow of his redemptive power. The power does not ebb, we reverse it. God will never force redemption on anyone. "Behold, I stand at the door and knock. . . ." If the very heart of sin is self-attention, we cannot blame God or accuse him of inadequacy when we go on attending first to ourselves and refuse him even our recognition.

Every person on earth has the potential of being "complete in him" and yet we cling to incompleteness. God's heart is open to everyone, but the guilt cannot fall on those who have not heard this glorious truth. It must fall on us who have heard and have refused it, have not acted. The mountainous carts of food we buy in our supermarkets will nourish no one but ourselves if we load it in our cars and stack it on the shelves of our snug, comfortable houses. We will eat and we will be nourished—we will be overweight—but what we have taken for ourselves will feed no one else. We *take* and we grow fat and prosperous and satisfied and we praise God for his goodness to *us*. We *take* what we understand at a superficial glance at Calvary and thank God for our own "salvation." We *take* solace from our church life, we *take* enough spiritual food from the Sunday sermon to last us a week. We Americans *take* the freedom from war on our own shores and bless the Lord for being so good to *us*.

We *take*.

And that is as far from what Jesus commanded as the east is from the west, the north from the south. He urged us to *take* one thing and one thing only: a cross. "And he that taketh not his cross, and followeth after me, is not worthy of me."

But, you ask, what of the free gift of eternal life in Christ? Are we not to take this? The question is in itself meaningless until we begin to see what the free gift really is. Of course eternal life is a gift

181

from God. We can do nothing of ourselves to earn it. But when will we see that we cannot learn to *live* eternal life until we have learned the cruciform truth of *giving?*

The Lamb of God could *take* the sins of the world only because he *gave* himself in the act. Enough has been written concerning the necessity for us to receive from God. We receive all the day long. We receive as we sleep at night. We receive from our friends and from our families and from our governments and from the wonderful working of our own physical bodies. We receive from our minds—every minute we receive from God through the gift of our memories—knowledge retained for our use because we have *remembered* how to use it. We must receive from God or perish, but our very receptivity turns stale unless we have learned to give as we have learned to receive.

I may be considered naïve by some, but I believe the child of God can learn to give as naturally as he receives. To give is not fully inherent in the human nature, but it is fully inherent in the nature of the Lamb of God. And when he comes to live his life within us, *giving* can become second nature to us.

"Worthy is the Lamb," we say, but we do not recognize the nature of the Lamb until we have joined him, however feebly, in *giving*. The theme of giving runs steadily through all Jesus said and did as he lived among us. "It is more blessed to give than to receive." We toss this off with the glibness of a motto. It is truth. It is *the* truth at the heart of re-demption. No one can truly begin to participate in the Great Giving of God until he has himself learned to give. The way to eternal life in the heart of God is open to anyone—"Come unto Me, *all* ye. . . ."

God plays no favorites, but who can truly *come* to the crucified One, putting a limitation on what he offers? "God is not willing that any should perish," but neither is he interested in merely "sav-ing" a few select ones from the misfortune of miss-ing out on heaven! He calls us all to himself, but inherent in the call is the poured-out life. Calvary is a fact. God has, in his Son, poured out his life for us. Are we to receive this poured-out life and tuck it away for our own eternal security? We blaspheme the very God we profess to worship when we do.

There are no inadequacies with God: Worthy *is* the Lamb. But ". . . he that taketh not his cross, and followeth after me, is not worthy of me." We feel somehow as though we are accentuating our humility when we go about declaring ourselves un-worthy of God. We will always be *other* than God. There is only one true God and our rightful place is at his feet. His ways *are* higher than our ways, his thoughts higher than our thoughts. But Jesus used the word "worthy" in connection with us. Quite clearly he said that *if* we are willing to take up our own cross, we would be worthy of following him. To take up one's cross means to be willing to give of oneself without stint or self-pity. To take up one's cross and follow Jesus means we will get up and go on when we fall, as he did when he stumbled and fell on his way to Calvary. Jesus was carrying his own cross, remember, and he stumbled and fell *three times*. When we have learned the cruciform way of giving ourselves, we will go on as he went on. We will not stop to admonish ourselves for being human enough to stumble and fall on the way. We will remember that our Master fell too, and, even as he fell, he *gave* to us. Even as he fell, he *gave* us the chance to learn that falling is not our problem; our problem is that we stay on the ground, horrified at our own lack of spirituality. The three falls of Jesus on his way to Golgotha are among his greatest gifts to us. In every act, he gave, and unless I am willing to diminish the power of God for those around me, I will come to him to learn how to give in every act of my own life. Can I bless someone by falling? Not, perhaps, by the fall itself, but I can give courage by going on after the fall, with my cross still on my shoulder. And from the third fall of Jesus, I can learn that if I am to be humble, as my Lord is humble, there will come times when I must be willing to let an outsider help me carry my heavy burden. The proud heart cannot bear to share its load, as Jesus shared his with the Cyrenian. If I am to come to him with my whole being, I will learn to give by sharing even my burdens. He offers himself constantly as a yokefellow with us all. ". . . my yoke is easy and my burden is light." Our burdens remain burdens, but they are lightened for us when we permit the Son of God to walk in the yoke with us. What we tend to forget is that he walks *in other people*. There are haughty Christians who refuse help from those whom they consider less spiritual than they. This spirit within us is not the Spirit of the Man-God who gladly allowed the stranger from Cyrene to help him carry his heavy cross. God became a human being in Jesus of Nazareth. His human body was exhausted and so, like us, he fell beneath the load of the heavy crossed timbers. He was the Son of God, but he was also the Son of Man, and he fell down on the rough stones of the street that led to Golgotha. Even as he accepted the help of the man pressed into his service, he *gave*. He was on his way to the ultimate, final demonstration of the redemptive love of his Father—on his way to save us all, and he accepted the help of a stranger.

Worthy is the Lamb, because he *gave*.

Worthy are we as his followers only when we are willing to learn to give. There is an eternal flow from the very heart of God and its motion is always outward. That flow comes to us steadily in his love, beginning with Creation and reaching us through the blood of his cross, holding us afloat in our time through the Spirit within us: God giving himself today as steadily, as freely as Christ gave at Calvary.

Worthy is the Lamb because he is still giving.

O Lamb of God, I come, I come.

We can only give to him by coming to him in response to his call. There is no other way. Just as there is no real giving to each other without giving of ourselves, so there is no giving to God that matters except the gift of our selves. And this—just as we are. We shudder at the prospects of such a twisted, scarred, hollow gift to be placed at the feet of the holy God of Love. And yet this is his way for us. And it is his way because it is the only way of reconciliation. We cannot alter our own lives. Only God can do this and just because we can't in our finite minds comprehend his wanting to does not change the *fact* of his longing toward us. The pure, holy, sinless Son of God longs over every calloused, ugly human heart, just as he longs over every grieving human heart, every broken and suffering human heart.

Why is it so difficult for us to see that God loves us because he cannot help it? Why is God's helplessness against love beyond our comprehension? Mainly, I suppose, because we are not capable of loving for long without some response from the loved one. God *is* capable. He can no more help loving us than he can change. And he cannot change. He is God.

He cannot change and he cannot stop loving and he cannot stop giving. Moment by moment the love of God is being pressed upon us, urged upon us. We worthy of him? When we very occasionally experience an awareness of this love always coming toward us, we want to hide and cry: "No, I can never be worthy!" Perhaps we can never be worthy of God's love, but Jesus said we could be worthy followers of his, *if* we would enter into the great redemptive act with him. If we would take up our crosses and follow him. But before we attempt this, we should take a long look at where he walks. Where Christ goes, the company will be mixed, unlike us. There will be those who are, according to our thinking, beneath us. Where he goes there are those whom we choose to label racially or socially or intellectually or spiritually inferior. There are the criminals where Jesus goes and the self-righteous religionists and the prostitutes and the radicals. He walks his earth still, the Good Shepherd, in search of *everyone* who needs him and this is everyone everywhere in every condition of life.

We cannot walk with God only here and there. We try, and then when we lose sight of him, when we no longer hear his voice, no longer sense his presence, we cry out: "God has left me!" He has, in a sense. He has walked on to where the need is. God can never be satisfied as we are satisfied with walking only the streets of upper-middle-class suburbia. He can never be satisfied with walking the city streets only in front of high-rise apartments with doormen. He can never content himself with walking only the carpeted or marble aisles of churches. He walks all these places, but he always goes on to where the need is not so well-dressed, not so fragrant of cologne and good tobacco and furs.

God walks on.

And we are being called continuously to walk with him. But we lose sight of him when he goes on as he always will to a place where we don't feel at home. We keep "those people" in "their places," but the Lamb of God knows those places and he loves those people as much as he loves us.

We are all invited. We can all come. God cannot help loving everyone, but because he loves, he moves. And he moves toward everyone, giving of himself. Anyone can join him at any time, but he is not waiting to hear us say merely: "O Lamb of God, I come, I come." He is waiting for us to *come*. There is one first sign that lets him know we mean it, and that is the gift we bring. The only one we can ever bring that will matter to the God of love: ourselves. And "Oh, wonderful, wonderful!" we are free to bring our selves, we are urged by the Lamb of God to bring them—*just as we are*.